HIKING THE WEST COAST OF VANCOUVER ISLAND

TIM
LEADEM

. . .

HIKING *the*
WEST COAST
of VANCOUVER ISLAND

GREYSTONE BOOKS

Douglas & McIntyre Publishing Group
Vancouver/Toronto/Berkeley

Greystone Books
A division of Douglas & McIntyre Ltd.
2323 Quebec Street, Suite 201
Vancouver, British Columbia
Canada V5T 4S7
www.greystonebooks.com

Library and Archives Canada Cataloguing in Publication
Leadem, Tim
Hiking the west coast of Vancouver Island / Tim Leadem.
Includes index.
ISBN-13 978-1-55365-024-9   ISBN-10 1-55365-024-7
1. Hiking—British Columbia—Vancouver Island—Guidebooks.
2. Trails—British Columbia—Vancouver Island—Guidebooks.
3. Vancouver Island (B.C.)—Guidebooks. I. Title.
GV199.44.C22V35 2005   796.51'09711'2   C2005-900019-8

Library of Congress information is available upon request

Editing by Naomi Pauls
Cover design by Peter Cocking
Text design by Jessica Sullivan and Peter Cocking
Cover photograph by Jerry Kobalenko / First Light
Photos by Adrian Dorst and Tim Leadem
Maps by Clover Point Cartographics Ltd. and Grafische
Printed and bound in Canada by Friesens
Printed on acid-free paper that is forest friendly (100% post-consumer
recycled paper) and has been processed chlorine free.
Distributed in the U.S. by Publishers Group West

We gratefully acknowledge the financial support of the Canada
Council for the Arts, the British Columbia Arts Council, and the
Government of Canada through the Book Publishing Industry
Development Program (BPIDP) for our publishing activities.

CONTENTS

PREFACE AND ACKNOWLEDGEMENTS *vii*

INTRODUCTION *1*

1   Coastal Hiking *9*

2   The Juan de Fuca Marine Trail *29*

3   The West Coast Trail *45*

4   Carmanah Walbran Provincial Park *77*

5   Long Beach and the Tofino/Ucluelet Area *89*

6   The Nootka Trail *109*

7   Cape Scott Provincial Park and Area *125*

8   Natural History *145*

9   First Nations *153*

10 Conservation *157*

FOR FURTHER READING *169*

INDEX *173*

Near Bonilla Point, West Coast Trail

PREFACE AND
ACKNOWLEDGEMENTS

. . . . .

This guidebook just kept growing. For many years, I edited and later authored a guidebook to the West Coast Trail. Over the years, though, I have hiked many other trails on the wet west coast of Vancouver Island (including all of the ones in this book) and I have long wanted to share them with others who enjoy exploring the wilderness.

For me, the question is always how to do this responsibly. I realize that by broadcasting the physical appeal and beauty of a place, something of its wildness may be lost as more people are attracted to experience the same landscape. However, I also understand that by promoting remote areas, they are more likely to be protected from development. That is the paradox: to conserve an untouched place, it must often be opened to human scrutiny in order to obtain the will to preserve it. Too often, though, some of the wild is rubbed away in the process.

I am a firm believer that people need untamed places for their souls. The sense of the spiritual that is in all of us is touched by these scenes—the swirling of the sea as it shoots up surge channels, the liquid emerald of a stream as it runs through a rocky gorge, the glint of the sun as it shines off a tiny fern in the dank humus of the forest floor. Perhaps we need these wild places just to be and not necessarily to be there for us. The many species that make up the forest ecosystem can survive quite nicely without us. There should be places on this globe where humans do not dare to tread.

Enjoy these hikes. Take in their incredible beauty and inexhaustible wonder, but leave these sacred places as you find them. Better still, do your part to ensure that we may know other wild places in our hearts if not with our eyes.

Wild Side Trail, Flores Island

Hikers who enjoy these trails—and I certainly include myself within this group—owe considerable thanks to the conservationists who had the foresight and fortitude to fight to preserve the lands upon which we walk. Humphrey Davy, Jim Hamilton, Hugh Murray, Karen McNaught, Ric Careless, John Willow and Gordy Price all pioneered the West Coast Trail and the hikes around Nitinat Lake in order to promote the area and conserve it. The Juan de Fuca Trail benefited from similar efforts from Sierra Club members Bruce Hardy, Chris Nation, John Newcombe and Greg Darms. The preservation of the Carmanah Valley is due largely to the hard work of the Western Canada Wilderness Committee. A large chunk of the Walbran Valley has been saved from clear-cut logging through the combined efforts of several environmental groups, including the Carmanah Forestry Society led by Syd Haskell.

For their many helpful comments and suggestions while I was writing this guide, I thank the employees of Pacific Rim National Park Reserve and BC Parks. Similarly, I am grateful to the many hikers along the way who offered commentary. To hiking companions, past and present, who share the scenery and sometimes the travails of the trail, may the path rise up to greet you and may the wind be ever at your back. I especially thank Susan Bates for her companionship on many of these ventures.

I also thank Naomi Pauls and Lucy Kenward, two fine editors at Douglas & McIntyre, for their suggestions and critiques. All mapping was done by Clover Point Cartographics, and I particularly thank Taryn Musgrave and Jeff Warwick for their efforts. Chris Berg of Grafische and Julian Anderson were helpful in sorting out technical software problems with the maps.

Since conditions along these trails are constantly changing, neither the author nor the publisher guarantees the accuracy of the information in this book. You must allow for the unexpected.

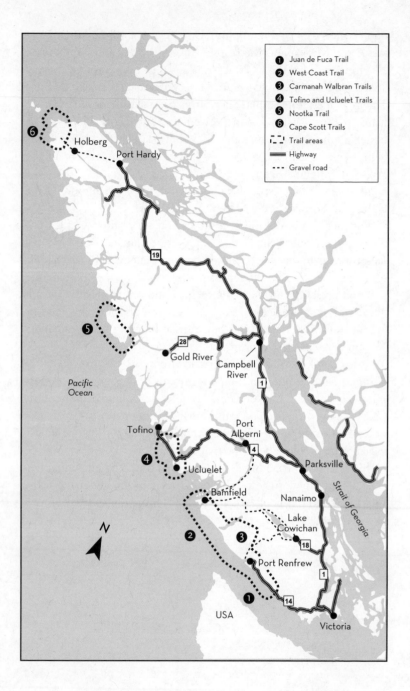

①	Juan de Fuca Trail
②	West Coast Trail
③	Carmanah Walbran Trails
④	Tofino and Ucluelet Trails
⑤	Nootka Trail
⑥	Cape Scott Trails
⌐ ¬	Trail areas
▬▬	Highway
- - -	Gravel road

Holberg

Port Hardy

19

⑥

⑤

28

Gold River

Campbell River

1

Pacific Ocean

Tofino

Port Alberni

④

Ucluelet

4

Parksville

Bamfield

②

Nanaimo

③

Lake Cowichan

Strait of Georgia

18

Port Renfrew

①

1

14

USA

Victoria

N

INTRODUCTION

. . . . .

The west coast of Vancouver Island is a special place. It affords the hiker some of the most beautiful and secluded beach walks anywhere in the world. The terrain varies, from beaches of white sand that stretch as far as the eye can see to sheer rocky cliffs to flat-as-pavement sandstone shelves that extend far out into the sea at low tides. Hikes along this coast, particularly the longer treks, are events to be savored.

This book was written to serve a number of purposes. A certain amount of planning is involved in any long hike. People who wish to walk Vancouver Island's west coast trails will find some tips and hints here. Many users of this book will not have experienced coastal hiking before, so there is some advice on making your hike an experience to be treasured rather than a disaster. Chapters on the specific trails include detailed information about access, trail features and historic points of interest. At-a-glance highlights at the start of each chapter or trail description provide distance breakdowns, time estimates, difficulty ratings, and other useful information. Finally, it is a rare hiker who is not interested in the natural history or human history of an area. This book is not meant to slake that thirst but rather to whet the reader's appetite for more knowledge.

> ## ABOUT THE MAPS
Relevant topographic maps for a trail are listed at the start of each chapter. The 1:20,000 maps are Terrestrial Resource Inventory Management (TRIM) maps produced by the Government of British Columbia and are available from Clover Point Cartographics in

Victoria, www.cloverpoint.com. Unless otherwise noted on the maps that supplement the text, these are the base maps used to depict the location of trails. The 1:50,000 maps are produced by the federal government as part of the National Topographic System. For information on obtaining these maps from map dealers, visit the Natural Resources Canada Centre for Topographic Information Web site, maps.NRcan.gc.ca.

> ## FINDING AND READING TIDE TABLES

For most of the hikes discussed in this book, you will want to consult a tide table. All tide tables are now available on-line from the Canadian Hydrographic Service (CHS) Web site, www.waterlevels.gc.ca. You will need to find the closest station to your hike to select the appropriate tide table. For ease of reference, these stations are provided in the highlights box for each hike where tides are an important factor.

The Pacific regions you will need to consult include Zone 9—Sooke, Zone 11—Port Renfrew to Tofino, Zone 12—Nootka and Zone 15—Cape Scott. When you click on the relevant map area, you will see the zone number at the top of your web browser. You then choose a station from the pull-down list. If you do not have access to Internet service, you may use the CHS's toll-free number, 1-877-775-0790. Follow the prompts until you reach British Columbia. Information is available for the following areas discussed in this guide: 1. Botanical Beach, 7. Long Beach and 8. Winter Harbour. More information is available on the Web site than by telephone, so for the most accuracy, you should consult the tide tables on-line.

Tide tables are still available in print, and the relevant ones for the west coast of Vancouver Island are published in volume 6 of *Canadian Tide and Current Tables*, available from bookstores and usually found in the boating and shipping sections.

If you are not familiar with reading tide tables, here are a few pointers. Tide tables are given for all stations on a daily basis. Here is an example of what a tide table looks like for a given day. (This one is from the Bamfield station.)

TIME PDT	HEIGHT M	HEIGHT FT
02:00	3.2	10.5
08:07	0.7	2.3
14:17	3.3	10.8
20:35	0.6	2.0

In most 24-hour periods there will be two changes of tides, so there will be a high tide (also called a flood tide) followed by a low tide (also called an ebb tide) followed by another high and then a low. A tide table gives the height of the tide in meters and in feet. For those of you used to tides being listed only in Standard Time, note the recent change to Pacific Daylight Saving Time (PDT). When hiking along the shore in summertime, you no longer need to add an hour to tide tables. Also note that for most 24-hour periods there will be a low tide that is lower than the other low tide. This is called the lower low water (LLW), while the other low tide is termed the higher low water (HLW). The same is true for the high tides, with the two daily high tides known as the higher high water (HHW) and lower high water (LHW). On some days there will be only three tides in a given 24-hour period.

Should you need more precision than that provided by the usual tide tables, consult the on-line chart that shows tidal predictions for a station on an hourly basis.

Pay attention to tides when planning your hike. For example, using the chart given, if you know you have to get around a headland that is passable at low tide near Bamfield, and it is about 2 kilometers (1.2 miles) from your campsite, you would be wise to rise early and start out on your trek so that you arrive at the headland at the lowest ebb of the HLW tide. If you know it will take an hour for you to hike the 2 kilometers, you should start out no later than 7:00 a.m. to arrive at the headland at 8:07 a.m., when the tide is lowest.

But you will not always be hiking so conveniently close to a tidal station. In this common situation, you should interpolate a time between stations to predict the tide at your proposed destination. Suppose you are on the West Coast Trail south of Tsusiat and you want to hike through the Hole-in-the-Wall near Tsusiat Point. The next station to the south for which there is a tide table is Port Renfrew, and its tide table for the same day as the previous example is as follows:

> **2004-09-16 · THURSDAY**

TIME PDT	HEIGHT M	HEIGHT FT
02:08	2.8	9.2
08:17	0.9	3.0
14:32	2.9	9.5
20:55	0.9	3.0

By comparing the charts, note that the difference in the morning low tide between Bamfield and Port Renfrew is +10 minutes. If you examine a map of the coast, you will see that Tsusiat Point is about one-third of the way between Bamfield and Port Renfrew. Thus, if you want to arrive at Hole-in-the-Wall at the lowest point for the morning low tide, add about 3 minutes (10 minutes divided by one-third). So you should plan on being at Hole-in-the Wall at 8:10 a.m.

Keep in mind that tides have a progression pattern, so you will have some leeway afforded to you, and it is a rare situation where you will have to be extremely accurate with your prediction. However, it is good practice to try to be as accurate as possible in working out your tide predictions because sometimes your safety may depend upon your precision. Also always keep in mind that it is much safer to hike along the shore on an outgoing tide than on an incoming one.

> **RATING SYSTEM FOR TRAILS**

One of the more difficult questions to answer is "How hard is the trail?" Terms such as *easy, intermediate* or *difficult* convey only relative, often subjective, information. What may be easy for the experienced trekker may be quite difficult for the novice.

I have examined several trail rating systems in the belief that the best ones should yield as much objective information as possible, allowing you to maximize your pre-hike planning and training.

Throughout this book, I use a trail rating system to convey the degree of difficulty you can expect on any given hike. I have modified the internationally used Volkssport rating system to make it more relevant to coastal hikes. The original Volkssport system, which emphasizes degree of incline, is detailed in the following table:

> **VOLKSSPORT TRAIL RATING SYSTEM**

PART 1—INCLINE

1 Very little hill climbing

2 Some moderate hill climbing

3 Some significant hill climbing

4 A good deal of significant hill climbing

5 Many steep hills or a high-altitude trail

PART 2—TERRAIN

A Almost entirely on pavement

B A significant part of the hike is on groomed trails, with very little difficult terrain

C A significant part of the hike is on somewhat difficult terrain (rocky/rooted paths)

D A significant part of the walk takes place on very difficult terrain

E The majority of the walk takes place on very difficult terrain

Although elevation gain is a factor in some coastal hikes, it fails to connote the true difficulties that can be encountered in such hiking ventures. Coastal hiking in this part of the world involves trying to stay on the beaches as much as possible. The reason for this becomes obvious to hikers once they encounter the impenetrable rain forest that hugs the coast of Vancouver Island. And yet not all beaches are equal. A beach of slippery boulders is much more difficult to traverse than one of densely packed sand or flat sandstone shelf. Some of the hiking also takes place away from the shoreline. In areas of impassable headlands, one is forced to hike through the forest. With these factors in mind, I have developed the following system to grade the difficulty of the hikes described in this book:

> **TRAIL RATING SYSTEM USED IN THIS GUIDE**

PART 1—INCLINE

1 Few elevation changes

2 Moderate elevation changes; may include use of stairs on some sections

3 Some significant elevation changes, some use of ladders, some use of ropes as aids over steep sections

4 Significant elevation changes involving ladders or artificial aids such as ropes

5 Many steep sections with many ladders up steep cliff areas

PART 2—TERRAIN IN FOREST

A Almost entirely on pavement or boardwalk in good shape

B Groomed trails or boardwalk in moderate shape

C Significant portion of trail on difficult terrain, roots or rocky paths; presence of mud during wet conditions

D Significant portion of trail on very difficult terrain; muddy quagmires

E Majority of hike on very difficult terrain and/or muddy quagmires

PART 3—TERRAIN ON BEACH

I Fairly flat beach walking on sandstone or hard-packed sand

II Beach walking on loose sand or small pebbles

III Beach walking on smallish-sized rocks

IV Beach walking on slippery boulders of large size; some moderate rock scrambling

V Beach walking mainly on extremely slippery, very large boulders or scrambling on difficult terrain

The following list may help you to choose a hike from the book based upon your experience and the time available to you.

Easy Hikes for Novices (easy day hikes)
Juan de Fuca Trail—Botanical Beach and Mystic Beach
Middle Carmanah trails in feature zone
Wild Pacific Trail
Willowbrae Trail
South Beach Trail
Nuu-chah-nulth Trail
Schooner Cove
San Josef Bay, Cape Scott Park
Ronning Gardens

Intermediate Hikes (long day hikes)
Juan de Fuca Trail — Parkinson Creek to Sombrio
Cape Beale Headlands, near Bamfield
Walbran Valley Trails
Wild Side Trail, Flores Island
Raft Cove

Intermediate Hikes (multiday)
Juan de Fuca Trail — Botanical Beach to Sombrio Beach
West Coast Trail — Pachena Bay to Nitinat Narrows
Nootka Island Trail
Cape Scott

Advanced Hikes (multiday)
Juan de Fuca Trail
West Coast Trail
Lowrie Bay, Cape Scott Park

> **TIME ESTIMATES**

The problem with giving time estimates is that the time to walk a set distance varies for individual hikers. Times also tend to be heavily dependent upon weather and trail conditions. Thus the times given in this guide are meant to be averages. They are not meant to be standards to beat or match. Note the time it takes you to complete a section, then use the estimate as a basis of comparison for future portions of the hike. On the few trail sections with incoming tides, you should be extra careful with your time planning. For these sections, allow for extra time to ensure that if something goes wrong, you have a chance to get to safe, higher ground. Because of the risks it is strongly suggested that you should hike these sections of the trail only on an outgoing tide.

The hikes described in this guide are listed from southern Vancouver Island to the north. Before you head out on any of these hikes, there are a few things you should know about coastal hiking, and these are covered in Chapter 1.

COASTAL HIKING

. . . . .

Hiking along the beaches and coastal trails of west Vancouver Island may be unlike anything you have ever experienced. Coastal hiking is a unique genre of hiking, which can range from some of the easiest trekking you will ever encounter to some of the roughest. Much of what you experience will depend upon two factors you won't be able to control: the weather and the tides. If you are lucky enough to have sunny weather, many of the trails through the forest will dry out. Instead of negotiating slippery roots and deep mud holes, you can breeze through and wonder what all the fuss is about. Or if you hike when the tides are low, you will find stretches of level, easy walking along either sandstone shelf or densely packed sand. If you miss the low tides, you will often find your beach route blocked by incoming seas, which under adverse conditions can become life-threatening. This chapter is meant as a general guide to some of these conditions and offers some tips on improving the quality of your hike.

> **PRACTICAL ADVICE**
There is more to hiking than having the proper gear and the right maps. Hiking the majority of the coastal trails in this book involves traveling through wilderness. A certain "wilderness ethic" is required for camping. Your aim should be to leave no trace of your passage through the pristine beauty. The adages "Pack it in, pack it out" and "Take nothing but photos; leave nothing but footprints" apply to the trails in this guide. Therefore you must practise no-trace camping. You should consider camping without building a fire. Unless you need to keep warm or dry out some of your gear, there is little sense in constructing a fire on the beach.

Ladders at Logan Creek, West Coast Trail

Hiking in the wilderness involves a good dose of common sense. Some of the trails in this guide are not heavily used during the summer, and all of the trails described here are seldom visited in the winter. Thus you should always advise close friends or relatives of your itinerary and expected date for finishing a hike. The number of rescues on the West Coast Trail alone has increased dramatically over the past few years, and often injuries are caused by hikers hurrying. Although the West Coast Trail can be hiked in a few days, there is no need for such speed. The enjoyment of a wilderness setting is a part of the experience. None of the hikes described in this book are meant to be endurance tests or competitive races. Take the time to observe nature and enjoy the experience.

Leaders of a group have a special duty to ensure that everyone sticks together. The slowest members are usually the least experienced and the most likely to encounter accidents or injuries. Everyone should be properly equipped and prepared to deal with emergency situations.

Probably the greatest danger to poorly equipped or inexperienced hikers is hypothermia, a term that means "low body temperature." It is especially likely to occur when dampness is combined with cold, a situation for which the west coast of Vancouver Island is well known, even in midsummer. You can get so cold that your body's normal means of regulating temperature, such as blood vessel contraction, shivering and fast respiration, all fail. If you reach this point, your presence of mind also fails and you are prone to making bad decisions instead of taking the drastic action necessary to restore body heat. An early symptom of hypothermia is prolonged shivering. The later, more serious symptoms are connected with the loss of self-control: poor muscle coordination, weakness, slurred speech and impaired judgment. From this juncture, it is downhill to coma and death unless appropriate action is taken immediately.

The best treatment for hypothermia is prevention: being equipped with adequate rain gear and warm clothing. If someone in your party does experience hypothermia, rescuers must remember that a person suffering from hypothermia has lost the ability to generate body heat and must be supplied with heat from an external source. This source could be the warmth from a campfire, gently inhaled steam, warm (but not scalding) liquids or another person's body heat. Merely wrapping a person in warm clothing or a sleeping bag may be useless—an innocent mistake that has cost lives.

Coastal hiking also involves the diurnal cycle of tides. Throughout this book reference is made to hiking along the beach if the tide is low enough. Tide tables are critical reference guides for hiking the coast. If predicting tides is vital (for example, when hiking a stretch of coast where you could be trapped by an incoming tide), you should interpolate from tides at given stations to your own location.

At several locations along the coast, you will have to cross a stream on foot. If the stream is fast flowing, a staff or hiking poles are essential for balance. High-quality sandals will help you negotiate the slippery rocks you will likely encounter in stream crossing. If there is a possibility of being swept out to sea, use ropes and send one hiker across at a time. If everyone moves into the water at once, there is a danger that if one person falls, the entire group may be swept out to sea.

Remember, too, that the trails in this guide are home to some large land mammals—cougar, black bear and wolf. Of the three, the black bear is the most common critter and the one you are most likely to meet. You can avoid potentially dangerous situations if you follow a number of precautions:

> Always make noise in an area frequented by bears. Wear bear bells, clap or talk loudly.

> Do not approach or feed bears or any other wild creature. Do not provoke them either.

> Store all of your food in caches high in a tree or in metal caches where they are provided. Do not store any food or toiletries in your tent. Bears tend to be nocturnal creatures and have been known to invade tents in search of food that is inside. Avoid the use of perfumes and colognes and insect repellent sprays that emit a fruity or sweet odor.

> If you encounter a black bear on the trail, back away slowly. Do not turn your back on the animal. Do not run away or wave your arms at it. Try to avoid eye contact. If a female black bear attacks you in order to protect her cubs (a defensive attack), then you should play

dead until she decides that you are no longer a threat to her. If a black bear stalks you and then attacks you (an offensive attack), do not play dead. You should fight back and use whatever weapon is available to fend off its attack. Bear spray and bear bangers are two devices that may prove useful in avoiding an attack.

> Avoid cubs at all times.

The same warnings apply to cougar encounters, with some exceptions. Keep eye contact with the cougar at all times and never turn your back on it. Do not crouch but stand up and try to appear as large as possible. A cougar is an elusive creature, and likely the big cat has seen you and fled the scene before you are even aware of its presence.

Wolves are sometimes encountered along the Nootka Trail. If you should see one, do not feed it or encourage it to approach. The wolf is a wild creature and is not like your pet dog. Always maintain eye contact with a wolf and ensure that you do not habituate it to human ways. The same warning is valid for cougars and bears: these creatures, once accustomed to humans, lose their innate fear and are capable of causing harm.

Finally, for many of the hikes listed here, information boards at trailheads will display information about recent sightings of bears, cougars or wolves. Take note of these locations and exercise caution in the areas frequented by these wild animals. If you travel with a dog, keep in mind that a dog may be attractive prey to bears, cougars or wolves and may bring the danger back to you. Dogs are not allowed on the West Coast Trail.

> **PERSONAL CAUTIONS**

Before hiking any of the trails described in this book, you should be aware of some of the potential problems you may encounter. Here are ten pieces of advice gleaned from thirty-plus years of coastal hiking experience.

1. *Respect the sea.* It is unbelievably powerful and can catch you unawares. The worst danger is from occasional freak Pacific swells—or rogue waves, as they are sometimes called—tumbling up a surge channel or rising dramatically over rocks or the sandstone

shelf. People have been plucked off rocks and carried out to sea by these sudden swells. Rogue waves may occur during high or even low tides. They are difficult to predict and pose a danger to the unsuspecting hiker.

There are a few particularly hazardous areas that you will hike through. One such dangerous spot is Nitinat Narrows, where you may be temporarily marooned if there is no one available to ferry you across. Very fast currents mixed with ocean breakers have caused some deaths there. Crossing streams and rivers on foot on an incoming tide can be treacherous. The incoming sea acts as a dam to the outflow of water from the stream. This pooling effect means that the water levels are not only deeper but also subject to counter currents from the tide. If you arrive at a stream during this phenomenon, it is better to wait until the tide has turned before forging across. Finally, and this can't be repeated enough, be aware and wary of tides. More than one camper has set up a tent well away from the sea at low tide only to awake to find tent and gear awash and afloat in the middle of the night. Another serious situation is hiking the shore at low tide and finding your progress barred by a cliff or surge channel and your return barred by an incoming tide. Always carry with you tide tables that cover your area and days of travel.

2. *Respect rocks, cliffs, slippery rocks and logs, and the sandstone shelf.* There are hazards on all parts of these trails. Slips on logs or rocks may result in serious injuries that require evacuation. On some parts of the coastal trails, you are one step away from a long drop. Pay particular attention to your feet placement when taking photographs from the top of cliffs. A lot of time the vegetation may be deceptive and actually overhang the cliff face. If your hiking boots lack good traction, the dangers are multiplied. A heavy pack can also increase the danger of a fall.

Many of the hikes listed in this guide feature boardwalks in sections or ladders or stairs in steep areas. The condition of these structures may vary. Be particularly vigilant of rotten wooden structures or missing rungs or planks. To cross rotting boardwalks, step on two planks at the same time or, if possible, walk along the log supports. If the walk is tilted, you should either walk off the boards if there is space or walk along the lower edge of the walkway, nearer to the

Cable car, Camper Creek, West Coast Trail

ground. If the boards are slippery, it may be safest to walk off the boards altogether. Maintaining a medium speed allows you to keep going forward instead of down should a board break.

On some hikes there will be ropes that someone has left behind as an aid to ascending or descending a cliff face or steep section. Unless you have personally placed the rope there and can vouch for its security, you should test the rope before you absolutely need to rely upon it. This may mean giving it some tugs and placing some weight on it before you begin your ascent or descent.

Some of the rougher routes and trails in this book use logs or fallen trees as makeshift bridges over streams and creeks. There is a certain skill and art involved in getting across log bridges safely. Walk on the very crown of the log and try to get as much of the tread of your sole onto the log as possible. Be particularly wary of logs that are losing their bark. The bark may slough off and carry you with it. Balance is critical in a successful log cross. If you are intimidated by the prospect of crossing a slippery log poised 10 meters (32 feet) above a rushing stream, you should practise on beached logs where a loss of balance will not carry severe consequences.

Finally, before crossing a deep stream, first loosen your pack straps so that you can shed your pack in the event that you do fall into the water. Hikers have been drowned by the weight in their packs after slipping from a log into rushing water.

3. *Be prepared for rain.* Even during the summer months, you may encounter bad weather on the west coast of Vancouver Island. Within hours a front may move in, bringing cold air, strong winds and torrential rains. Rain gear is one of your most important pieces of equipment and should be adequate to keep you and your sleeping bag dry. Most packs are not waterproof, so use a pack cover or store your clothing and sleeping bag inside the pack within waterproof sacks or bags. A tent with a waterproof fly is also a necessity. You should know the meaning and symptoms of hypothermia, a condition that can sneak up on you and is the leading cause of death among amateur hikers. (See page 11 for a discussion of hypothermia.)

4. *Be properly equipped.* Once on these trails, you may be some distance from the end and any guaranteed source of supplies. You should be self-sufficient, with enough food and fuel to last the duration of your planned trip.

5. *Wear comfortable, sturdy hiking boots.* Next to rain gear and a waterproof tent, good boots with adequate ankle support are the most critical items for safe hiking.

6. *Carry enough water containers.* There are parts of the coast where, in a dry summer, you might hike for several hours without finding water sources. You will be losing a lot of internal fluids from perspiration and exercise, and it is important to keep hydrated. Regrettably you must now carry a water purifier to make water from many of the streams and creeks along coastal trails safe to drink.

7. *Carry a stove for cooking.* On the coast, heavy rainfalls may make it difficult to start a fire. Also, fires along coastal trails are restricted to the beach area. A stove is also required for all camping in the Carmanah Walbran Provincial Park, since campfires are not allowed in wilderness campsites.

8. *Carry a well-stocked and current first-aid kit.* Be knowledge-able about the items in the kit to be able to use them in an emergency.

9. *Take special precautions if hiking off-season.* The off-season period is generally regarded as the time between October and April. Conditions along the longer, remote trails are likely to be severe, and rescue services are limited. Those who do decide to hike in the off-season and require search-and-rescue services must be prepared to wait for help and to pay for any rescue operation, including the cost of helicopter evacuation. Stream crossings in the off-season are also subject to high levels due to runoff from torrential rains. It may be impossible for you to get across several streams. In particular you should be aware that the ferry services that operate on the West Coast Trail in the summer are not in effect during the off-season.

10. *Get experience first.* With the exception of some of the trails listed for Tofino and Ucluelet, these trails should not be your first hiking experience. You will encounter most or all of the following: mud, slippery logs, slippery rocks, washouts, high streams, high tides, sudden ocean surges, drop-offs, steep banks, windfalls, overgrown sections, darkness, high winds and downpours. If you are not com-fortable with encountering any of these elements, you should proba-bly not attempt these hikes. If, however, you are willing to rough it and adapt to what the weather may throw your way, by all means pre-pare well and go ahead.

Reading this guide is not a substitute for experience. Remember that trail conditions change every year. Winter storms topple trees across the trails or wash out sections.

> ## ENVIRONMENTAL CAUTIONS

If ten thousand people pass through an area in a season and each person does a little damage to the environment, the result is a lot of damage. If each hiker does no damage, however, the result will be no damage. It is easy to visit an area, use it and enjoy being there, but leave behind no sign of your visit.

1. *Pack out all of your garbage.* The rule for all wilderness hik-ing is "If you can pack it in, you can carry it out." This rule applies to all tin cans, food packages, bottles, clothing, plastic bags and poly-ethylene sheets. Burying your garbage is not a solution, given the

Log crossing, Nootka Trail

number of people who use the trails and the non-biodegradable nature of most garbage. Burnable garbage should be thoroughly burned, both for aesthetic reasons and to avoid attracting animals to campsites. Human solid waste should be properly buried or deposited in the intertidal flush zone. Use the outhouses where provided, but do not leave garbage in them.

2. *Camp with care.* When setting up your campsite, use an area that obviously has already been used. Do not hack a new site out of the bush. If you are beach camping, camp below the winter high-tide line and, of course, well above the summer high-tide line.

3. *Keep creeks clean.* Confine bathing and using soap for washing dishes to areas downstream of camping and any water supply

intake. Use biodegradable soap or, better yet, no soap at all. Instead use sand and small rocks to scour pots and pans.

4. *Respect all private lands.* You will pass by or through private lands on many of the hikes described in this book. Some lands belong to First Nations and are clearly marked as Indian reserve lands. On the West Coast Trail, Native guardians patrol all reserve lands. No camping or trespassing is allowed on these lands—you must remain on the trail. Over the years lands and buildings belonging to Native people have been vandalized and damaged. All reserve lands are clearly marked on the maps in this book.

5. *Consider other hikers.* Remember that large groups have a greater environmental impact on a trail than small groups and a greater social impact on other campers. On the West Coast Trail, Parks Canada staff restrict group size to ten. Many of the more popular camping spots along the coastal trails, such as Tsusiat Falls or Calvin Falls, become quite crowded. In these areas it is important to recognize that some hikers may have a different schedule for hiking than you. Some may rise early to catch the low tide; others may want to sleep in to recover from the inevitable aches and pains of back-packing. Keep others in mind and keep the noise level down when you are in camping areas.

6. *Don't dine out.* Refrain from taking any sea life, such as mussels or clams, for personal consumption. In addition to a problem with red tide, sea life is not easily replenished when so many hikers are traveling along the coast.

7. *Leave nature be.* Do not remove any wild creature or touch sea life that you may find in a tide pool. This warning is for your own safety as well as that of the animal. Certain sea life have stinging cells that may leave you with a rash or burning sensation on your skin. Respect the wildlife that you meet along the way. Do not feed any wild creature since you may unwittingly habituate it to human contact with potentially negative consequences to it.

> **EQUIPMENT AND PROVISIONS**

For many backpackers there is perhaps no topic more controversial than what type of equipment to use for a hike. Hikers have been known to hold discourse for hours on the relative merits of synthetic versus natural fill in sleeping bags or the functionality and comfort of packs. The advice given here is not about such choices but about the selection of adequate gear and food to enable you to be self-sufficient on your hike. Whether you plan to hike one of the longer trails, such as the West Coast Trail, or to take a day trip along the Wild Pacific Trail, you should plan and be prepared for any emergency or weather condition that is likely to arise on your trek.

Lack of proper equipment can turn a pleasurable hike into an ordeal. Weather along the west coast can range from cold winds and heavy rains to hot, bone-dry, sun-baked days when small streams have all disappeared. Most of the really bad weather occurs during the winter, but summer hikers should still expect rain. Your gear, in particular your footwear, must also be suited to the terrain you are likely to encounter. Wet and slippery logs, rocks and boardwalks; muddy paths; fogged glasses; and vertical ladders that seem to go on forever are all part of the coastal hiking experience. Once again, if you are prepared for these encounters, they will be challenges rather than potential sources of injury or illness.

The backpacker's challenge is to keep down the weight without sacrificing any of the items and foodstuffs that are essential for an enjoyable trip. As a general rule, you should carry no more than one-third of your body weight. This rule depends a lot on your age and physical shape. Experience in hiking is also a valuable asset that weighs nothing but usually sees one through the hardest going. Note that many of the hikes described in this book (with the exception of those in the Tofino/Ucluelet area) are for the experienced hiker, not the novice.

What you will need to carry for an extended backpacking trip can be broken down into five categories: general equipment (the hardware necessary to protect you from the elements), clothing, cooking and eating utensils, food and optional gear. I have not included any brand names, since personal tastes differ so widely. I would, however, urge you to purchase or rent only high-quality gear that can withstand the rigors of the trail. Since you will be carrying everything you bring, I also urge you to go with lightweight but dependable gear. The following lists are intended as a guide.

> GENERAL EQUIPMENT

○ pack (waterproof or with waterproof pack cover)
○ waterproof stuff sacks or heavy-duty garbage bags
○ tent (with waterproof fly)
○ sleeping bag (synthetic fill preferable to down)
○ insulating sleeping pad
○ ground sheet or tent footprint (optional—depends on make of tent)
○ fire-starting kit (explained in text below)
○ multipurpose knife/tool set
○ repair kit (for clothes, tent and pack)
○ 15 meters (50 feet) of 7-millimeter rope
○ tide tables
○ flashlight or headlamp (with spare batteries)
○ candles (for light and for starting a fire)
○ compass or GPS
○ water-resistant or waterproof watch
○ maps
○ first-aid kit (essential)
○ insect repellent (essential in summer)
○ sunscreen
○ toiletries
○ day pack (optional)
○ cash (for ferry crossings and Indian reserve crossings)
○ walking stick or hiking poles (optional)

Sharing some of these items can lighten individual loads. If you are hiking in a large group, however, be sure that there is adequate equipment for the entire group.

There are many types of backpacks on the market. You should compare them and consult someone experienced in backpacking before purchasing one. Most packs are not waterproof, so you should either purchase a cover for your pack or stow your food, sleeping bag, sleeping pad and clothing in stuff sacks or heavy-duty garbage bags before placing them in your pack.

Sleeping bags with synthetic fill are better than down-filled ones since they absorb less moisture and dry more quickly. Your sleeping bag should have a waterproof stuff sack and be effective to approximately 0°C (32°F).

The fire-starting kit should consist of waterproof matches and/or butane lighters plus fire-starter material. Some form of fire starter (waxed wood sticks work really well, or use the stub end of a candle) is essential, since much of the wood along the trail may be wet. Place a candle stub or a small tea candle under a tepee of kindling and let the candle burn until the wood catches.

You can assemble a small repair kit consisting of needles and thread for repairing cloth. For repairing your pack, take along a couple of meters of flexible wire and lightweight pliers. (A multipurpose tool usually functions equally well.) Your repair kit should also contain some heavy string and duct tape.

The rope is used for caching food at night. In some areas bear caches will already be in place. At other sites you will have to select a spot to cache your food in a place inaccessible to bears and rodents, such as up a tree. Many hikers use a carabiner to attach food sacks to the rope.

Plastic bags (self-closing ones are best) are also useful for storing items in your pack and keeping matches and toilet paper dry. A flashlight or headlamp with spare batteries comes in handy for those evenings when you are trying to pitch your tent in the dark. The headlamps with LEDs are particularly good, since they weigh very little and the battery lasts a long time. Candles with a good candle lantern are good for that warm glow in the tent for reading.

Your first-aid kit should be well stocked for a long hike. There are several commercially prepared kits, or you can make up your own. First-aid knowledge and training is important to obtain before your trip.

A small container of insect repellent is essential during the summer. Biting insects are usually not plentiful on the beach; when you walk away from the sea breezes, however, you will discover that there are indeed mosquitoes and black flies along the coast. The repellent should contain DEET to be effective. If you want to "go organic," try eating garlic instead of using chemicals. I do not vouch for its effectiveness, but you may find that if you ingest enough, you won't be bothered by pests of either the six-legged or the two-legged variety.

Logan Creek suspension bridge, West Coast Trail

Sunscreen with PABA or zinc oxide as the blocking agent should be carried if you are either an optimist or a sun lover or both.

A light day pack or fanny pack is useful if you plan to establish a base camp and take day trips from it. A walking stick or a collapsible hiking pole is useful for most of the terrain you will encounter along coastal trails. These items are invaluable along slippery boardwalks and help maintain balance during stream crossings. Many hikers use a pair of poles, particularly those who suffer from knee ailments.

> CLOTHING

- ○ hiking boots (waterproofed in advance)
- ○ spare socks
- ○ gaiters
- ○ trousers (preferably fleece, wool or fast-drying)
- ○ hiking shorts
- ○ waterproof outerwear
- ○ waterproof hat (with wide brim for both sun and rain)
- ○ underwear
- ○ long-sleeved shirts or T-shirts
- ○ wool sweater or fleece jacket
- ○ gloves (optional for summer months)
- ○ good-quality sandals (for stream crossings)
- ○ sunglasses

Clothing should be chosen for utility, warmth and weight. Some hikers prefer to put on a set of clean clothes every morning, whereas others will wear the same clothes every day and thus leave room in their pack for optional items such as a book or a camera. Footwear is perhaps the most critical item on this list. The wearing of inadequate footwear such as runners or light hiking boots causes most of the injuries along coastal hikes. Knee injuries are most frequent, closely followed by ankle injuries.

Boots should provide good ankle and arch support. Vibram soles or the equivalent are probably the best for the many types of terrain on coastal trails. Your boots should be well broken in and water-proofed before you start. All outdoor stores stock a number of brands of waterproofing agents to match the composition of your boot. Split leather (suede) boots are not recommended, since they are difficult to keep waterproofed. You should also carry a pair of high-quality sandals (*not* flip-flops or leather sandals) or reef shoes for stream crossings and use around the campsite. These should be well con-

Boulder beach, Nootka Island

structed, with strong Velcro straps, and should provide good traction on slippery rocks.

Proper socks can help prevent blisters. Thin socks worn as inner liners wick away perspiration and help cut down on chafing. Outer socks are heavier and should be padded in the heel and toe area for extra comfort. You can expect to have wet feet along the trail unless you wear a good pair of gaiters. These should be high quality and have a strap for securing them under the insoles of your boots. Waterproof material for the lower portion combined with a breathable water-resistant material for the upper part of the gaiters work best.

Wearing jeans while hiking is strongly discouraged. When wet, jeans become heavy and lose their ability to insulate. Choose a quick-drying pair of pants or fleece tights, or simply wear shorts under waterproof pants.

Rain gear is essential. Take along a loose-fitting jacket and a pair of trousers that have side zips long enough to allow you to put them on without first removing your boots. The choice of material for such a rain suit is one of the more controversial issues relating to gear selection for any backpacker. You should consult a number of knowledgeable people and read articles that compare products (often found in magazines such as *Backpacker*) before purchasing your rain gear. The choice is between material that is waterproof, which keeps you dry but clammy, and material that is breathable, which eliminates internal moisture but may allow leaking during the pelting torrents of rain that frequently occur on the coast.

A wide-brimmed hat is a good addition to your backpacking wardrobe; it will keep the sun off your face and the rain out of your eyes. Some hikers take along a toque for chilly nights.

The principle of layering is very effective for the variable climate of the west coast. Wearing several layers of warm, lighter clothing instead of a single layer of heavy clothing allows you to take off or add layers as the weather changes.

A fleece jacket is warm, sheds water and dries rapidly. Such a jacket is an excellent choice in either a zip-up or pullover style. Trousers and socks made out of fleece material are also good choices for warm clothing. Once again, you must choose between being warm but carrying the extra weight of several articles of clothing and traveling light but possibly being cold.

> COOKING AND EATING UTENSILS

○ stove (essential)
○ fuel
○ pots
○ cup
○ plate or bowl
○ fork and spoon
○ knife (a general-purpose pocketknife is good for both food and trail use)
○ plastic garbage bags
○ pot scrubber and biodegradable soap
○ water filter or water-treatment system
○ water bottles or containers

Although campfires are permitted on the beaches of the coastal hikes, you cannot always rely on a fire for cooking. A lightweight stove that burns white gas (naphtha petroleum) and has a pump system is thus an essential item on your equipment list. Be sure to bring enough fuel. Most hikers warm up some hot water in the morning for tea or porridge. Remember that dinners take longer to cook than other meals. Estimate your fuel consumption for the number of meals you will be cooking, then add extra fuel to be sure you will not run out.

The larger the group size, the larger the number and size of pots you should take along. For small groups (four or less), you can get by with two pots—a 4-liter (1-gallon) pot and a 2-liter (1/2-gallon) pot are usually adequate for most purposes. If you are a gourmet cook, you will probably want to check out the backpacking utensils available at most outdoor stores. Everything from a backcountry oven for baking bread to a wilderness espresso maker is on the market. Consider that each one of these items means additional weight to your burgeoning pack.

Water filters are now widely used to deal with increasing problems with the quality of water from streams. The presence of *Giardia lamblia*, a micro-organism that may cause stomach cramps and diarrhea, is suspected in some of the streams along the coast. Other streams are beginning to show the presence of the bacteria *Escherichia coli (E. coli)*, which can also cause health ailments. Thus you should boil your water, treat it with chemicals or filter it. Some bodies of water, such as the Nitinat Narrows, Cheewhat River, Klanawa River and Walbran Creek, are brackish and unsuitable for drinking. Boiling such water does not purify it but rather makes it more saline.

As a general rule you should treat all water sources along the coast. During the summer, you will probably be perspiring during a hike. Hydrating your body is critical to your well-being. Several hydration systems available on the market allow you to drink water while motoring along the trail. Carry a large collapsible water container for use at campsites or in case you need to carry water for some distance due to streams drying up in the summer.

> **FOOD**

Planning and some ingenuity are the critical ingredients in producing satisfying and economical meals on the trail. Lightweight freeze-dried food is available, but it tends to be expensive. A visit to the pasta or rice sections of the supermarket should give you some indication of what is available for dinner along the trail. You should try to find items that are light in weight and take little cooking time. In order to replenish your calories lost to exercise, you should stock up on carbohydrates and high-energy foods. In addition to meals, you will want to carry trail foods such as energy bars and trail mix. In planning your group meals, remember to pack sauces, spices and seasonings. Most hikers build up enormous appetites, so plan on extra food consumption. Always carry an extra day's worth of meals in case you run behind your intended schedule as a result of unforeseen difficulties.

> ## OPTIONAL GEAR

What you take besides the necessities depends on your experience, strength, pack size and interests. You may wish to take along a compact camera to visually record your journey. Digital cameras are particularly useful since you can take lightweight memory cards rather than rolls of film. A small pair of binoculars is also useful for observing wildlife such as sea lions and whales offshore. You can usually find room in your pack for a good book or deck of cards if you are so inclined.

Inveterate anglers will want to bring along fishing rods; a compact spin casting rig is most suitable. You will need a licence for both tidal and freshwater fishing for many of the areas covered by this guide; you can obtain them from most outdoor stores. A Parks Canada fishing licence is required for fishing in Pacific Rim National Park Reserve.

If you have read this far, heeded the cautionary advice and crammed your pack full of gear that you know how to use, then there's nothing left to do but hit the trails!

2

THE JUAN DE FUCA
MARINE TRAIL

· · · · ·

> **TOTAL DISTANCE:** 47 km (29 miles)

> **TOTAL TIME:** 4–5 days

> **AVERAGE RATING:** 3 C II

> **ACCESS:** Highway 14 (from Victoria)

> **HAZARDS:** Tides, boulders, creeks, cliffs, black bears

> **SPECIAL FEATURES:** Sea stacks and other rock formations, suspension bridges, beach walks, tide pools, waterfalls, whales, sea lions

> **MAPS 1:20,000:** 92C049 (Sombrio Point) · 092C050 (Jordan River) · 092C058 (Port Renfrew) · 092C059 (Parkinson Creek) **1:250,000:** 92C08 (Jordan River) · 92C09 (Port Renfrew)

> **TIDE TABLES:** Zones 9 and 11. Use Sooke tide tables for the first part of the hike and tables for Port Renfrew for the sections near Botanical Beach.

> **SECTIONS AT A GLANCE**
> *China Beach Trailhead to Bear Beach*
> DISTANCE: 10.5 km (6.5 miles) · TIME: 6–8 hours · RATING: 3 C III
> Expect mud in all but the driest of summers

> *Bear Beach to Chin Beach*
> DISTANCE: 10.5 km (6.5 miles) · TIME: 6–8 hours · RATING: 4 D II
> Numerous elevation changes to get across streams

> *Chin Beach to Sombrio Beach*
> DISTANCE: 8 km (5 miles) · TIME: 4–6 hours · RATING: 4 C II
> Elevation changes

> *Sombrio Beach to Parkinson Creek*
> DISTANCE: 8 km (5 miles) · TIME: 4–6 hours · RATING: 3 B III
> Note current access problem at West Sombrio Bluffs

> *Parkinson Creek to Botanical Beach Trailhead*
> DISTANCE: 10 km (6.5 miles) · TIME: 5–7 hours · RATING: 2 B II
> Some elevation changes

> **ACCESS AND PERMITS**

Access to the trailheads for the Juan de Fuca Marine Trail, which skirts the coastline south of Port Renfrew, is straightforward. All trailheads are accessed off Highway 14, which runs roughly west from Victoria to its terminus in Port Renfrew. All trail access points are well marked by signs posted on the highway. If you are hiking in a group, allow some time to arrange cars at your planned destination. You will reach the first trailhead, at China Beach, a few kilometers after you pass through Jordan River, an easy two and a half hours' drive from Victoria. Use the first parking lot on the right as you exit the highway. You will reach the next trailhead, at Sombrio Beach, after you cross the bridge over Loss Creek. An old logging road takes you downhill to a parking lot.

The trailhead at Parkinson Creek is a few kilometers to the west of the Sombrio Beach trailhead. A logging road of approximately

4 kilometers (2.5 miles) takes you to a parking lot. You will intersect a number of logging roads on the route to this lot. Generally keep to the right at these intersections. To reach the Botanical Beach trailhead, travel through Port Renfrew. Turn left before you arrive at the Port Renfrew Hotel and the government dock. You will drive along a gravel road for approximately 3.5 kilometers (2 miles) before you reach the large parking lot for Botanical Beach and Botany Bay. All trailheads have large covered information boards that list valuable information such as tide tables and bear and cougar sightings.

Hikers have reported a growing problem with theft and vandalism to vehicles left in parking lots at some of the trailheads.

Bus transportation to the trailheads on the Juan de Fuca Trail is available from Victoria on the West Coast Trail Express. A daily shuttle bus stops off at French Beach, China Beach and Port Renfrew. Further information and reservations are available by phoning 1-888-999-2288 or by visiting their Web site, www.trailbus.com.

At time of writing, hiking permits are not required for the Juan de Fuca Marine Trail. However, there is an overnight camping fee of $5 per person for each night you plan to camp on the trail. The permit can be obtained through a self-registration system from any of the trailheads. Fines may be assessed if you camp without a permit.

For up-to-date conditions on the trail and posted warnings, visit the BC Parks Web site at wlapwww.gov.bc.ca/bcparks/.

> TRAIL DESCRIPTION AND HISTORY

Like the West Coast Trail, the Juan de Fuca Marine Trail had its origins in the 1889 telegraph line constructed between Victoria and Bamfield. The line was constructed to link the British Empire through a transpacific cable station located at Bamfield. Later the telegraph line was replaced by a telephone line. At certain locations, linesmen were housed in cabins to patrol the line and ensure it was intact. Unlike the better-known and more popular West Coast Trail, however, the trail between Port Renfrew and Jordan River did not form part of the Life Saving Trail and thus disappeared for many decades.

There were, however, a number of shipwrecks along this stretch of the "Graveyard of the Pacific." Little remains of these wrecks now but for their names given to some of the creeks, such as Clinch and Ivanhoe, that you will cross along this trail.

As the West Coast Trail grew more popular and more crowded, a number of backpackers became convinced that alternative routes should be set aside for recreational hiking. In the 1970s, members of the Victoria Sierra Club began to lobby the provincial government to preserve the southern coast along the Strait of Juan de Fuca between Jordan River and Botanical Beach near Port Renfrew. At the same time, Victoria *Colonist* columnist Alec Merriman began promoting the preservation of Botanical Beach and other areas along the coast.

The Sierra Club launched various exploratory forays into the thick bush in an attempt to link some of the more popular beaches, such as Mystic and Sombrio. Unfortunately, logging companies began harvesting Crown land under forestry tenure in the area surrounding Sombrio Creek and Parkinson Creek. In the early 1980s, the Sierra Club launched its first civil lawsuit in a Canadian court in an attempt to forestall the logging. Although this legal action failed, the case was the first in a series of lawsuits brought by the Sierra Club that resulted in the formation of the Sierra Legal Defence Fund in Canada to promote the use of court actions to preserve wilderness in the province.

As a result of the efforts of the Victoria Sierra Club, the Capital Regional District set aside the "West Coast Strip," as it was called in those days, as a planned future park. In the 1990s, the provincial government saw the usefulness of preserving wilderness and recreational access to it and acquired the land base for the present Juan de Fuca Marine Trail.

The trail was set aside as a provincial park in 1995 as part of the Commonwealth Nature Legacy, created in conjunction with the holding of the Commonwealth Games in Victoria in 1994. The trail is 47 kilometers (29 miles) long and connects Botanical Beach at the west end and China Beach at the eastern terminus. It parallels provincial Highway 14, which links Victoria and Port Renfrew. The trail affords views of the Strait of Juan de Fuca, named for the Greek pilot who explored the strait in 1592. De Fuca, who was traveling from Mexico, is believed to have sailed as far as the Strait of Georgia that year. The trail also gives access to some of the more remote beaches on the southwest coast of Vancouver Island.

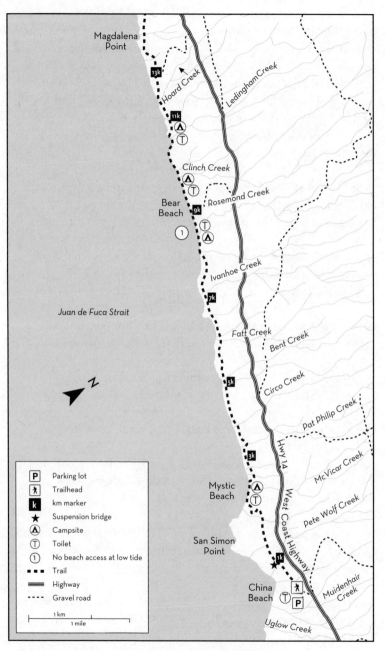

MAP 1: JUAN DE FUCA TRAIL—CHINA BEACH TO MAGDALENA POINT

Before beginning your hike, check the Internet site for BC Parks for up-to-date trail conditions (wlapwww.gov.bc.ca/bcparks). You should also consult tide tables, since there are many places where you must hike the beach and there are stretches of the coast not accessible at high tides. Tide tables are posted by BC Parks at all trail-heads. The tables for Sooke are good for China Beach and Mystic Beach; the Port Renfrew tide tables are good for Bear Beach to Botanical Beach. The following table lists the locations where you may encounter a tide problem:

(1) FROM CHINA BEACH: 8.7 km (5.4 miles), at Bear Beach west of Rosemond Creek
PASSABLE at tides below 3 meters (10 feet)

(2) FROM CHINA BEACH: 20.6 km (12.8 miles), at Chin Beach
PASSABLE at tides below 2.75 meters (9 feet). Cabin available at 20.5 km (12.7 miles).

(3) FROM CHINA BEACH: 21.3 km (13.2 miles), at Chin Beach West
PASSABLE at tides below 2.75 meters (9 feet). Best to use forest trail.

(4) FROM CHINA BEACH: 28 km (17.4 miles), at Sombrio Beach
PASSABLE at tides below 3 meters (10 feet)

(5) FROM CHINA BEACH: 29.3–29.9 km (18.2–18.5 miles), at West Sombrio Bluff
PASSABLE at tides below 2.6 meters (8.5 feet). The bypass trail over this section is currently blocked due to a slope failure. Please check with BC Parks for status of this bypass trail.

(6) FROM CHINA BEACH: 30.2 km (18.7 miles), west of West Sombrio Bluff
PASSABLE at tides below 3 meters (10 feet)

All beach access trails along the trail are marked by large orange-red fluorescent balls that are usually suspended high in trees adjacent to the access point.

Comparisons between the West Coast Trail and the Juan de Fuca Marine Trail are perhaps inevitable. The newer trail is shorter, more accessible and can be readily joined at several locations, so users can hike it in segments rather than as one long trail. Signage along the trail is excellent, with kilometer markers clearly indicating distance from the trailhead at China Beach.

Although you do not need a permit to hike the trail, you do need to register for overnight camping. Campfires are permitted only below the high-water marks on the beach. BC Parks staff advises that a permit system may be required in the future if the trail becomes crowded and more heavily used.

Ample parking is available at the turnoff to China Beach, the eastern trailhead. Expect the first part of the trail to be muddy except during dry spells in the summer. On weekends, the stretch to Mystic Beach is also apt to be crowded with day hikers. Just before the 1-kilometer marker, you will cross the well-constructed suspension bridge over Pete Wolfe Creek. The trail then heads down to the first campsite, at Mystic Beach, reached soon after the 2-kilometer point. Mystic Beach is a great place to picnic or catch a shower from the waterfall sliding over the sandstone cliff, which is to the east as you reach the beach. The black rocks to the east past the waterfall lead to San Simon Point, which cannot be reached on foot.

You must walk west along the beach for a short stretch to a well-marked beach access trail in order to rejoin the main trail. The trail between Mystic Beach and the next campsite, at Bear Beach, is confined mainly to the forest, with some ocean views along the tops of cliffs just to the west of Mystic Beach. Watch your footing in the areas by cliffs; there was a fatality in this area in 2004. You should encounter numerous small streams where you may fill your water bottle or relax in the shade. All the streams have good bridges.

After you cross Ivanhoe Creek, you will begin a gradual descent to Bear Beach. The small- to medium-sized rocks on the beach may be slippery if wet, making hiking there quite onerous. Numerous people have twisted their ankles on this stretch while hiking with a heavy pack.

Good camping is found at Rosemond Creek and Clinch Creek, farther to the west. Clinch Creek is named for the schooner

D.L. Clinch, which was wrecked near here in 1860. Note that there is a tide problem just to the west of Rosemond Creek. At high tides, the sea reaches the base of the sandstone cliffs and cuts off the rest of the beach to the west. If you encounter tides in excess of 3 meters (10 feet), you should plan to camp at Rosemond Creek or wait there until the tide drops. Tide tables are posted at the trailheads to help you plan your hike.

The last camping spot in the vicinity of Bear Beach is located just to the east of Ledingham Creek near the 10-kilometer marker. There are pit toilets along this beach and a good water supply from the creek.

The trail from Bear Beach to Chin Beach is the most difficult part of the hike. There are many elevation changes as the trail crosses numerous streams in this section. All of the streams drain Jordan Ridge, which is located to the north. During the rainy season (generally the off-season, although a few days of steady rain will have the same result), you will encounter a lot of mud. There are also few camping opportunities in this section until you reach Chin Beach itself. If you are really in a fix, there is a small place to pitch a tent near the bridge over Hoard Creek. A rough beach access trail near the bridge over this creek leads down to a small gravel beach, which floods at high tide.

You will pass by Magdalena Point and Arch Rock between the 13- and 14-kilometer markers, although the point itself is not visible from the trail. The trail stays mainly in the cedar-hemlock–Sitka spruce forest, offering glimpses of the sea now and then. After you pass the 19-kilometer marker, you will begin a gradual descent to Chin Beach. At the eastern entrance to this beach, the route is cut off by tides above 2.75 meters (9 feet). If you become trapped by an incoming tide, you can take shelter in a small cabin, complete with sunroom, located near the 20-kilometer marker in the forest above the beach access trail.

Chin Beach provides several good camping locations. As you walk west down the beach you will encounter a number of beach access trails. Depending on the tide, you may walk along the beach and through some interesting rocky areas until you arrive at the last access trail, which like all the others is marked with bright-orange fluorescent buoys. This trail curls up the west side of a small stream

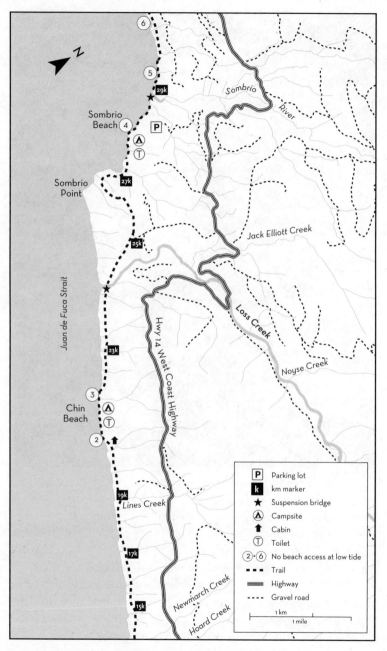

MAP 2: JUAN DE FUCA TRAIL—MAGDALENA POINT TO SOMBRIO BLUFFS

Green sea anemone, Botanical Beach

between the 22- and 23-kilometer signposts. If you miss this turnoff, you will reach yellow signs warning you that the beach route to Sombrio Point is impassable beyond here.

BC Parks designates the route between Chin Beach and Sombrio Beach as difficult. Once again, the difficulty arises because of the elevation changes required to cross a number of small streams. The highlight of this stretch of the trail is the suspension bridge across Loss Creek. From the centre of the bridge, you can view beautiful sea stacks seaward and a deep, rocky gorge in the opposite direction. After you cross this bridge, the trail climbs up and turns away from the coast to join an old logging road near the 25-kilometer marker. You will travel along this route for approximately 1 kilometer (0.6 mile), until the trail turns seaward and heads down towards Sombrio Point. You will be hiking at the top of a cliff with views to Sombrio Beach; stay well clear of the cliff face in this section.

From here, the trail hugs the coastline until you descend to east Sombrio Beach. There is good camping along this stretch of beach. At low tide, you can hike west along the beach to other good campsites in the forest above the pebble beach. To rejoin the Juan de Fuca Trail, look for it as it heads into the forest before you reach the squatter's cabin. In the past, a small community of rough cabins and sites hewn out of the bush dotted the entire stretch of Sombrio Beach.

In the summer, gray whales and the occasional pod of orcas may be spotted along Sombrio Beach. In the fall, the Steller's sea lion also will make its appearance along this coastline.

If you plan to stop your hike here, you will head away from the beach along a trail to a junction. The right fork leads to a large parking lot. From this lot a logging road snakes up the logged hill to connect with Highway 14. Sombrio Beach is a popular destination for day hikers, picnickers and surfers, and during the summer, especially on weekends; expect the parking lot to be full.

The left fork of the trail at the junction leads up to the suspension bridge over the Sombrio River, located just east of the 29-kilometer marker. Sombrio means "shady place" in Spanish. The river was named by Lieutenant Manuel Quimper, commander of the Spanish naval sloop *Princess Royal*, while on an exploratory voyage along the Strait of Juan de Fuca in 1790.

After you cross the bridge, you will hike down to join the beach. It is possible to hike along the beach at low tide all the way to Minute Creek. At high tide, there are bypass trails that you may take to get around the headlands. However, at present the bypass trail at kilometer 29.3 at West Sombrio Bluff is out of commission due to a slope failure. You will have to budget your time and hike this section at low tides only. The beach area here features large boulders, so plan to go slowly to get through these safely.

If you are hiking from Botanical Beach, the start of the bypass trail between the 30- and 31-kilometer markers is somewhat obscure. To reach it, hike a few meters up a small stream; the trail climbs up a slippery, muddy slope and is signed as a bypass trail.

Once past Sombrio River, you will be in newly cut forest for approximately the next 10 kilometers (6 miles) of the trail. The trail through the clear-cut can be muddy and slippery. Watch out for the numerous salal roots that criss-cross the trail at regular intervals. In this area during the late summer and autumn, you will probably see signs of black bear—usually in the form of scat festooned with salal berries. If you are hiking alone, it is a good idea to have a bear bell and to make some noise through the thick brush to warn any bears of your approach. Although BC Parks staff say there is no problem with black bears in this area, it is always wise to be wary and give them plenty of warning of your arrival. You should also store your food high in a tree.

If you have hiked the shore along the sandstone and conglomerate shelf, you will have to rejoin the trail before Minute Creek. This creek should be crossed on the suspension bridge located upstream, since crossing on foot at its mouth at incoming tides can be treacherous.

Midway between kilometer markers 32 and 33, you will pass through a grassy area with access to the shelf. At high tides, you will hear the rumbling of the surf in sea caves below the shelf. The campground at Little Kuitshe Creek is just past the 33-kilometer marker. Several tent sites have been hacked out of the salal and alder bush. A trail leads down to the coast with some good views back to Sombrio Point.

Kuitshe Creek at the 34-kilometer marker is a good stop for a rest. If you are experienced in rock scrambling, you can scramble down the left side of the waterfall downstream of the bridge and wade across the creek to reach Kuitshe Cove—a small but protected gravel beach. Alternatively, a small trail leads up from the bridge and then down to this small beach. The trail westward from Kuitshe Creek continues through new growth until you reach the parking lot at Parkinson Creek. A rough road that is passable in a passenger car leads up for approximately 4 kilometers (2.5 miles) to connect with

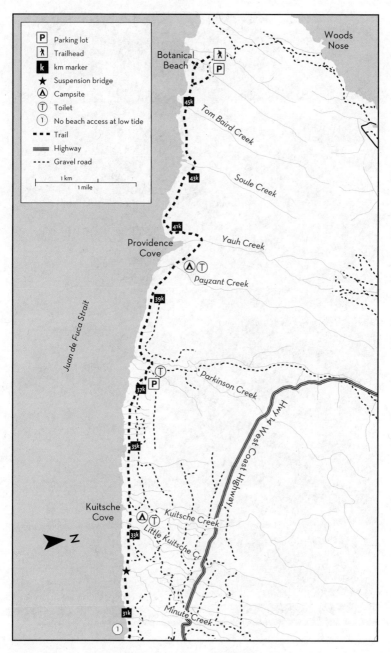

MAP 3: JUAN DE FUCA TRAIL—SOMBRIO BLUFFS TO BOTANICAL BEACH

Morning mist, Sombrio Beach, PHOTO BY A. DORST

Highway 14. If you are accessing the trail at Parkinson Creek, the road to the parking lot is well marked off Highway 14. You will intersect several other logging roads off the main road. Keep to the right as you descend to the coast to arrive at the parking lot.

The trail from the Parkinson Creek junction crosses two bridges; at the second one, Parkinson Creek Bridge, you will turn left to follow the creek for approximately 100 meters (330 feet). The trail then turns right, away from the logging road, to traverse through clear-cut and slash until you arrive at the coast again near kilometer marker 38. At that point, you may hike along the conglomerate shelf and explore tide pools, but watch for the orange buoys to regain the trail. After you pass kilometer marker 39 you will finally leave the clear-cut area and enter a mature cedar-hemlock forest. The going is much better here, with an abundance of boardwalks and plank walks to get you over the muddy parts.

An excellent campsite awaits you after you cross Payzant Creek at the 40-kilometer marker. Several tent platforms are set among the trees. The trail from here heads inland a bit so that you can cross Yauh Creek on a sturdy log bridge. Just past the crossing, you will reach a junction with a side trail leading to Providence Cove. The cove itself is worth a visit, although BC Parks discourages camping here. The campsites you see in this vicinity are former ones that were abandoned for the sites at Payzant Creek, which is named after Frederick Payzant, who went to the Klondike in the gold rush of 1898, failed to make his fortune, and retreated to a home near the mouth of this creek in 1903.

From Providence Cove the remaining 6 kilometers (about 4 miles) of trail become progressively easier as you approach Botanical Beach. Once you cross Soule Creek on a steel-girder bridge, you will hug the west side of Soule Gorge until you reach the coast. Soule Creek takes its name from Annie Soule. She was married to Tom Baird Jr., a son of Tom Baird Sr., one of the earliest settlers in the Port Renfrew area, who donated some of the land around Botanical Beach to the province for use as a park. From here, there are a number of unmarked beach access points as you hike to the west. The last 3 kilometers (about 2 miles) before Botanical Beach are in excellent shape, with boardwalks across most of the wet sections.

This section of the trail was built by youth from the T'souke and Pacheedaht First Nations. You cross Tom Baird Creek at its mouth by threading your way through a logjam—watch your footing in wet weather.

Botanical Beach is near the 46-kilometer marker. The beach is a great place for appreciating marine biology. It is best explored at tides below 1.2 meters (3.9 feet). The sandstone, conglomerate and shale rock has been eroded by the sea into many beautiful and unusual shapes, including amphitheaters, concretions and potholes in the sandstone shelf. The potholes may be observed at low tide and are a microcosm of marine life, containing anemones, coralline algae, sea urchins and starfish, to name just a few of the many species of organisms that are readily spotted. This area is a special protected zone, and it is illegal to handle or take any of the wildlife.

In 1901, the first marine biology station in the Pacific Northwest was built here by the University of Minnesota. Dr. Josephine Tilden founded the marine station, and for several years the site was home to groups of biologists who studied the marine flora and fauna. Over the years the station was abandoned, and its buildings have now been taken over by the thick rain forest. Many scientists, however, including a group of international botanists in 1960, have continued to assemble here to conduct studies in the biology of the area.

From Botanical Beach, you may continue up an old road for approximately 1 kilometer (0.6 mile) to the parking lot. As an option, you may continue along a shoreline trail that leads to Botany Bay and an access trail to the same parking lot. The parking lot at the Botanical Beach trailhead is quite large but is apt to be crowded on weekends.

3

THE WEST
COAST TRAIL

· · · · ·

> **TOTAL DISTANCE:** 75 km (47 miles)

> **TOTAL TIME:** 5–7 days

> **AVERAGE RATING:** 3 C II

> **ACCESS SOUTH END:** Highway 14 (from Victoria) or logging roads (from Honeymoon Bay), West Coast Trail Express bus **NORTH END:** Logging roads, MV *Lady Rose* or MV *Frances Barkley*, or West Coast Trail Express bus (from Port Alberni). Shuttle bus also serves Victoria and Nanaimo. Juan de Fuca Express water taxi (from Port Renfrew).

> **HAZARDS:** Tides, ladders, slippery boulders, cable cars, creek crossings

> **SPECIAL FEATURES:** Ocean views, bridges, lighthouses, sea caves, beach walks, wildlife

> **MAPS 1:20,000:** 092C057 (Vancouver Point) · 092C058 (Port Renfrew) · 092C066 (Whyac) · 092C067 (Carmanah Point) · 092C075 (Pachena Bay) · 092C076 (Tsusiat Lake)
1:50,000: 92C09 (Port Renfrew) · 92C10 (Carmanah Creek) · 92C11 (Pachena Point) · 92C14 (Barkley Sound)
A 1:50,000 map that covers the West Coast Trail is published by International Travel Maps in Vancouver, and is available from map

stores and outfitters. Perhaps the best map to take on the West Coast Trail is the one given out by the Pacific Rim National Park Reserve staff as part of your permit package. It is tear proof and rain proof so it travels well.

> TIDE TABLES: Zone 11. Use Port Renfrew tide tables for the southern half of the hike and Bamfield tide tables for the northern end.

> ## SECTIONS AT A GLANCE

> ### Gordon River to Thrasher Cove
DISTANCE: 6 km (3.7 miles) · TIME: 4–5 hours · RATING: 4 C.
Trail is all in forest

> ### Thrasher Cove to Camper Creek
DISTANCE: 8 km (5 miles) · TIME: 4–5 hours · RATING: 3 D V
The beach route from Thrasher is difficult until you reach Owen Point

> ### Camper Creek to Logan Creek
DISTANCE: 6 km (3.7 miles) · TIME: 3–4 hours · RATING: 3 D II
Considered the toughest part of the trail

> ### Logan Creek to Walbran Creek
DISTANCE: 4 km (2.5 miles) · TIME: 1–2 hours · RATING: 3 D II
Trail rather than the beach route is recommended

> ### Walbran Creek to Carmanah Creek
DISTANCE: 7 km (4.3 miles) · TIME: 3–4 hours · RATING: 2 D II
Can be done on the beach at low tides

> ### Carmanah Creek to Cheewhat River
DISTANCE: 10 km (6.2 miles) · TIME: 5–6 hours · RATING: 2 C II
Water sources may be a problem late in the season

> *Cheewhat River to Nitinat River*
> DISTANCE: 4 km (2.5 miles) · TIME: 1.5–2 hours · RATING: 2 C II
> All on inland trail. Possible to exit the trail at Nitinat River

> *Nitinat River to Tsusiat Falls*
> DISTANCE: 7 km (4.3 miles) · TIME: 3–4 hours · RATING: 2 C II
> Spectacular headlands and beaches

> *Tsusiat Falls to Tsocowis Creek*
> DISTANCE: 7 km (4.3 miles) · TIME: 3–4 hours · RATING: 2 C II
> Cable car across the Klanawa River. Very scenic. Valencia Bluffs,
> site of shipwreck

> *Tsocowis Creek to Michigan Creek*
> DISTANCE: 4 km (2.5 miles) · TIME: 1–2 hours · RATING: 2 B I
> Mostly on beaches

> *Michigan Creek to Pachena Beach*
> DISTANCE: 12 km (7.4 miles) · TIME: 4–5 hours · RATING: 3 B I
> Easiest part of the trail

> *Cape Beale Headlands*
> DISTANCE: 13 km (8.1 miles) round trip · TIME: 6 hours
> RATING: 2 D III
> Lighthouse passable only at tides lower than 1.8 meters

> *Keeha Bay*
> DISTANCE: 7 km (4.3 miles) round trip · TIME: 3.5 hours
> RATING: 2 D II
> Rough in parts but the beach is beautiful and deserted

> **ACCESS AND PERMITS**
Trail permits are required for all overnight stays on the West Coast
Trail between May 1 and September 30. Permit reservations are not
required for commencing the hike on weekdays during the shoulder

season (May 1 through June 14 and September 15 through September 30), since there is no quota system in place during those dates. Permit reservations for the peak season (June 15 through September 15) may be made by phoning the Tourism BC reservation service at the following numbers:

> 1-800-435-5622 within Canada and the United States
> 250-387-1642 outside Canada and the United States
> 604-435-5622 in the Greater Vancouver area

Reservations may be made seven days a week, starting April 1, between 7:00 a.m. and 7:00 p.m., Pacific Time, on a moving block-by-month system. If you wish to hike in June, you may phone the reservation number on April 1. For hiking in July, reservations are taken commencing on May 1. Reservations for hiking in August commence on June 1. Finally, if you plan to start your hike in September, the reservation system starts on July 1. There is a non-refundable fee of $25 per hiker for making reservations, which is payable by credit card (Visa and MasterCard only). Before you phone for a reservation you should know the following:

> date you want to commence your hike (with two alternative dates in case your chosen date is full)
> trailhead where you intend to start (Pachena Bay or Gordon River)
> mailing address of the group leader
> number of hikers in your group

The more popular dates for hiking fill up rapidly, so you should book as far in advance as possible. The maximum group size is fixed at ten persons. Only one commercial or organized group is permitted to start the trail every other day from either end of the trail.

You will receive a reservation confirmation number and a preparation guide when you register. Permits must be picked up at the Information Centre adjacent to your chosen trailhead before 1:00 p.m.

on the date of your hike. You may collect your permit one day in advance if you wish to get an early start on the first day of your hike. If you fail to claim your permit before 1:00 p.m. on the day you have reserved, your reservation will be automatically cancelled and your spot filled by someone on the waiting list.

There is a quota system in place. Only sixty hikers—thirty from Gordon River, thirty from Pachena Bay—will be allowed to commence the trail daily during the peak season and on weekends during the shoulder season. Five spots at each of the Gordon River and Pachena Bay trailheads are available on a daily basis for those who arrive without a permit. However, it should be noted that hikers who arrive at one of the trailheads without a reservation may have to wait several days for an opening during the peak season. Waiting lists for those without permits operate on a first-come, first-served basis. When you arrive at the trailhead, you should present yourself at the Information Centre in order to be placed on the waiting list. Spaces are then allocated by the staff at the Information Centres at 1:00 p.m. each day. All hikers must register and receive a one-hour orientation session at the trailhead before they are issued a trail use permit.

At this time the fee for obtaining a trail use permit is $90 per person. This fee is in addition to the reservation fee and is payable at the time the permit is issued. You will also pay the fees for ferry crossings across the Nitinat Narrows and Gordon River ($14 per person for each of these crossings at this time). You may pay by Visa, MasterCard, cash or traveler's checks in the exact amount only. The fee is charged to help defray some of the costs of maintaining the trail and for some rescue services. Day hikers are not assessed a permit fee. Hikers who attempt the trail without a valid permit may be forced to return and may face court charges.

For up-to-date information on waiting lists and permit requirements for the West Coast Trail, you may phone the following numbers:

> Pacific Rim National Park Reserve Headquarters · 250-726-7721

> Pachena Bay Information Centre · 250-728-3234

> Gordon River Information Centre · 250-647-5434

Tsusiat Point, Hole-in-the-wall

Transportation to and from the West Coast Trail, which runs
between the small communities of Port Renfrew in the south and
Bamfield in the north, can be a bit of a logistical problem to arrange.
Most groups leave a car at either end of the trail. If you do this, allow
a full day for travel. Alternatively, if you park your vehicle at a trailhead, you may use one of the shuttle services that are described
below to return to your vehicle.

The north end of the trail has better transportation facilities. The
MV *Lady Rose* and the MV *Frances Barkley* operate as ferries between
Port Alberni and Bamfield. At this time the vessels operate on a year-
round schedule, leaving Port Alberni every Tuesday, Thursday and
Saturday at 8:00 a.m. and reaching the Bamfield East dock at 12:30
p.m. They leave the Bamfield West dock at 1:30 and arrive at Port
Alberni at 5:30 p.m. There are additional summer sailings on Fridays
and Sundays from July 1 through Labour Day (the first Monday in
September). The Friday timetable is the same as the schedule given
above for Tuesdays, Thursdays and Saturdays. On Sunday the boat

departs Port Alberni at 8:00 a.m. and arrives at Bamfield at 1:30 p.m. The return voyage departs Bamfield at 3:00 p.m. and arrives at Port Alberni at 6:00 p.m. For further information and for reservations, which are highly recommended during the summer, call the following toll-free number during office hours from April through September: 1-800-663-7192. The local phone number in Port Alberni for Alberni Marine Transportation, which operates the *Lady Rose* and *Frances Barkley*, is 250-723-8313. If you take one of these vessels, note that you will still have an hour's hike to get to the trailhead.

The West Coast Trail Express is a private bus shuttle service to either the Pachena Bay or Gordon River trailhead. Its buses can transport up to twenty-four hikers and gear between Victoria, Nanaimo, Port Alberni and the trailheads. The shuttle operates daily between May 1 and September 30. For information, schedule and reservations, phone toll-free 1-888-999-2288 in Canada or visit their Web site at www.trailbus.com.

Finally, there is the Juan de Fuca Express, a water taxi that cruises between Port Renfrew and Bamfield. The service is run by Brian Gisborne, who is knowledgeable about the history of the West Coast Trail. If the weather and seas cooperate, you will be able to see many of the landmarks of the trail before or after your hike. For bookings and information, contact Trailhead Resort in Port Renfrew at 250-647-5468 or 1-888-755-6578 (toll-free in North America).

If you have your own transportation, you will need to use logging roads to reach the Pachena Bay and Nitinat Lake trailheads. All of the main logging roads are currently open to the public twenty-four hours a day, but loaded logging trucks have the right-of-way. Expect to encounter logging trucks if you travel on weekdays between 6:00 a.m. and 6:00 p.m. You should drive with your headlights on at all times. Remember also that logging roads are not well-maintained highways. You should expect to encounter blind corners, potholes and other hazards. No overnight camping is permitted on company-administered forestland except at designated camping sites.

Access to the Pachena Bay trailhead starts about 5 kilometers (3 miles) before Bamfield along a short branch road to the left off the main road. There is a sign for the West Coast Trail at this location. If you arrive at a bridge over the Pachena River, you have missed the turn. Parking is available in the lot at the end of this side road. Do not leave valuables in your vehicle; thieves have been known to operate in this area. Bamfield has a few grocery stores, restaurants and motels. Fuel can be purchased at a few locations. Camping is available either near the trailhead on the beach or at the commercial campground on Pachena Bay on the Huu-ay-aht Reserve.

Access to Port Renfrew, at the trail's southern end, is from Victoria via Highway 14 through Sooke and Jordan River. Alternatively, you can reach Port Renfrew through Lake Cowichan and a logging road system that starts just after Honeymoon Bay. The logging road from Shawnigan Lake through the San Juan Valley to Port Renfrew is currently closed because of a washed-out bridge about midway along the route. To reach the Information Centre and southern trailhead for the West Coast Trail, turn right before you reach the town site of Port Renfrew. You will cross the bridge over the San Juan River and go through the Indian reserve. The Information Centre is located on the south bank of the Gordon River. There are limited hotel and motel accommodations in Port Renfrew, but there are a number of bed and breakfasts. If you plan to camp, the Pacheedaht First Nation has some camping sites and RV sites for rent on the reserve near the Information Centre. Should you wish to camp in town, a campsite run by Trailhead Resort is located close to the government dock. Trailhead Resort also operates a store that carries hiking and camping supplies in case you forgot something.

> **TRAIL DESCRIPTION AND HISTORY**

For more than one hundred years there has been at least some semblance of a trail along the west coast of Vancouver Island between Pachena Point and Port Renfrew. The trail was first hacked out of the wilderness in 1889 for a telegraph line connecting Victoria with Bamfield, the western terminus of the first transpacific telegraph cable, which was meant to connect the British Empire. The old cable station in Bamfield is now the Bamfield Marine Sciences Centre, established for study into marine biology and ocean science for five western Canadian universities. Bamfield was named after William Banfield, a federal Indian agent who resided there. A gazetteer misspelled his name on one of the maps produced by

Cheewhat River bridge

Canada and the mistake has withstood time. In 1862 Banfield met a mysterious end by drowning; he is believed to have been murdered.

In 1906 the wreck of the SS *Valencia*, north of the mouth of the Klanawa River, took the lives of 136 people and had only 37 survivors. After this tragedy, the federal government conducted an inquiry, which resulted in several recommendations to improve the safety of seagoing vessels. One of these recommendations resulted in improvements to the rough path put up by the stringers of the telegraph line so that it could serve as a lifesaving trail for survivors of shipwrecks. It then became known as the Life Saving Trail, or the Shipwrecked Mariners Trail. Over the past two centuries, a number of ships have foundered along this stretch of the coast, giving it the name the "Graveyard of the Pacific." In 1911 the trail was designated a public highway and was allotted the standard-sized right-of-way of 66 feet. The federal government took on the responsibility of maintaining the trail. Cabins were also built at strategic locations, and line workers were stationed in them to patrol the trail and the telegraph line to ensure it was kept in operation. Remains of one of these cabins may be seen today along the trail at the Klanawa River.

As long ago as 1926, when the land in British Columbia seemed infinite, the recreation potential of Nitinat Lake and the coast was recognized, and a park reserve was established. This reserve was lifted in 1947 because the federal government considered the region too remote for recreation. A struggle broke out within the forest industry for control of the land base. First the area was set up as the Clayoquot Cutting Circle, where small, independent operators could work. But the major logging companies wanted to harvest the timber in the area through large commercial clear-cut operations.

After World War II, trail conditions deteriorated and the federal government temporarily abandoned the trail in 1954. Interest was rekindled in the 1960s when members of the Sierra Club began to hike and upgrade the trail. The Sierra Club also began intensive lobbying to have the trail set aside as a national park. In response, the federal government began to upgrade portions of the trail. Improvements continued in the 1970s—mostly to the northern section. The upgrade was completed by 1983, and the trail was formally established as the West Coast Trail Unit of Pacific Rim National Park Reserve (PRNPR) in 1993.

Responding to the increased use of the trail and to the shift in the type of people hiking it, the Canadian Parks Service carried out a program of repairs to the West Coast Trail in the 1980s to eliminate many of the obvious dangers and inconveniences. In the 1990s the provincial government added large tracts of land in the Carmanah-Walbran watersheds as well as a southern extension to the West Coast Trail—the Juan de Fuca Marine Trail. The result has been a vast increase in the number of hikers and backcountry users.

The West Coast Trail is relatively easy to hike in its northernmost section, from Pachena Bay to Walbran Creek. To the south, from Walbran Creek to Port Renfrew, the hike is relatively safe but not necessarily easy; there are still dangers for the unwary hiker. Whereas the trail is still a challenge to the average hiker, it is no longer the true wilderness it once was. For many, this change is distressing because it removes a challenge that cannot easily be replaced; for others, however, it means the opportunity to experience an area they may have been reluctant to enter a few years ago. One negative aspect of change, though, is the increased spoiling of the land caused by the carelessness or ignorance of hikers uneducated in trail courtesy and camping etiquette. This problem will only get worse unless every hiker develops a personal sense of stewardship for the land.

The trail may be hiked in either direction. Traditionally, the hike has been described from the south or the Port Renfrew trailhead to the northern terminus at Bamfield. Many people prefer to hike the trail in this direction to get the southern, more difficult part over with when they are still fresh. There are others, however, who prefer to hike the easier northern section while their packs are heavy and full of food and to break into the trail gradually. The decision is yours. For the sake of tradition, this book describes the trail as one proceeds from southeast to northwest. Where hikers proceeding in the opposite direction need to be aware of a particular problem, I have included this fact in the notes and trail description that follow.

Before beginning the trail, you must report to one of the trailhead Information Centres to pick up your trail use permit and to complete a mandatory orientation session given by a PRNPR staff member. Up-to-date information on trail conditions, any known problem areas and the tidal conditions you can expect for the duration of your trip is dispensed by knowledgeable staff. You will also be shown a fifteen-minute video presentation that describes what you may expect along the way. If you wish to get an early start in the morning, you should pick up your permit and complete your orientation the day before you begin your hike. The following table lists locations where you may encounter a tide problem.

(1) THRASHER COVE TO OWEN POINT
PASSABLE at tides below 1.8 m (6 feet). Allow lots of time to get around Owen Point. First access trail past Owen Point is about 1 km (0.6 mile) along the sandstone shelf, near marker 66 on the trail.

(2) OWEN POINT TO SECOND BEACH ACCESS TRAIL FROM SANDSTONE SHELF EN ROUTE TO CAMPER BAY
PASSABLE at tides below 2.4 m (8 feet). Difficult surge channel between second and third beach access trails. Many hikers elect to regain the trail at second beach access.

③ SECOND BEACH ACCESS TRAIL TO THIRD BEACH ACCESS
PASSABLE at tides below 1.7 m (5.5 feet). Difficult surge channel.

④ CAMPER BAY TO SANDSTONE CREEK
PASSABLE at tides below 1.2 m (4 feet). Difficult access trail along the side of Sandstone Creek. Not recommended for novices or at all for hikers going from Pachena to Port Renfrew.

⑤ LOGAN CREEK TO WALBRAN CREEK
PASSABLE at tides below 1.7 m (5.5 feet). Dangerous surge channel at Adrenaline Creek.

⑥ WALBRAN CREEK TO VANCOUVER POINT
PASSABLE at tides below 3.7 m (12 feet). Passable only when Walbran Creek can be forded.

⑦ VANCOUVER POINT TO BONILLA POINT
PASSABLE at tides below 3.7 m (12 feet). Beach is the usual route.

⑧ CRIBS CREEK TO DARE POINT
PASSABLE at tides below 2.1 m (7 feet). Difficult surge channel about 1 km (0.6 mile) before Dare Point. Beach route is not recommended.

⑨ TSUSIAT POINT
PASSABLE at tides below 2.7 m (9 feet). Hole-in-the-Wall. Bypass trail is available.

⑩ KLANAWA RIVER TO TRESTLE CREEK
PASSABLE at tides below 3.7 m (12 feet). Beach is the usual route.

⑪ TSOCOWIS CREEK TO DARLING RIVER
PASSABLE at tides below 2.7 m (9 feet). Beach is the usual route.

To enter the trail at the southern end, you need to take the ferry across; the Gordon River is too deep and wide to wade. On the eastern side of the river, the land belongs to the Pacheedaht First

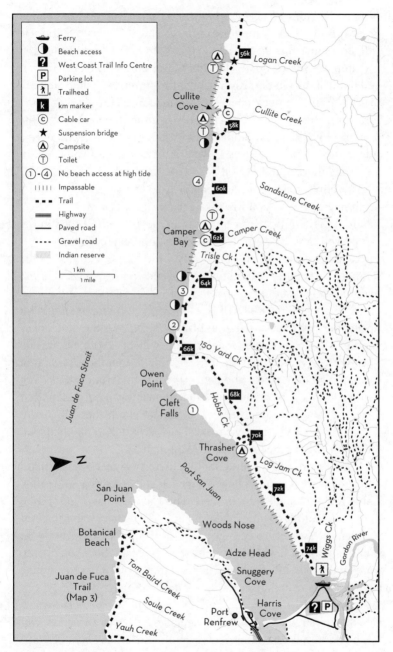

Legend:

- 🛶 Ferry
- ◐ Beach access
- ❓ West Coast Trail Info Centre
- Ⓟ Parking lot
- 🚶 Trailhead
- **k** km marker
- ⓒ Cable car
- ★ Suspension bridge
- Ⓐ Campsite
- Ⓣ Toilet
- ①-④ No beach access at high tide
- ||||| Impassable
- ••• Trail
- ═══ Highway
- ─── Paved road
- --- Gravel road
- ▨ Indian reserve

1 km
1 mile

Logan Creek

Cullite Cove

Cullite Creek

Sandstone Creek

Camper Bay

Camper Creek

Trisle Ck

Juan de Fuca Strait

150 Yard Ck

Owen Point

Cleft Falls

Hobbs Ck

Thrasher Cove

Log Jam Ck

Port San Juan

San Juan Point

Woods Nose

Adze Head

Botanical Beach

Snuggery Cove

Tom Baird Creek

Juan de Fuca Trail (Map 3)

Wiggs Ck

Gordon River

Soule Creek

Harris Cove

Port Renfrew

Yauh Creek

MAP 4: WEST COAST TRAIL—GORDON RIVER TO LOGAN CREEK

Nation. The present operator of the ferry service across the Gordon River is Butch Jack, a member of the Pacheedaht First Nation. He will ferry you across the river from the reserve. The ferry service will not drop off or pick up at Thrasher Cove; thus, all hikers will start and finish at the Gordon River. Under the current schedule Jack will pick up from the dock near the Information Centre at 9:00 a.m., 10:30 a.m. and 2:30 p.m. If you are hiking from the north end of the trail, there is a float you should hoist to alert the operator you need a ride across the Gordon River. Wait at the dock until you see him arrive and then lower the float.

The current schedule for pickup from the small dock on the north side of the Gordon River is 9:15 a.m. and 5:15 p.m.

From the Gordon River to Thrasher Cove, the trail stays in the forest, well away and up from the coastline. The coastal route is impassable because of cliffs. Any difficulties you encounter on the southern part of the trail will mainly depend on the weather. If it has been rainy, you should expect mud of varying depths, and all log crossings and boardwalks will be slippery. The hiking is mostly on up-and-down terrain or flat ground. When you pass the old donkey engine, a relic of earlier logging, you will be about halfway to Thrasher Cove. Note that the forest around the southern portion of the trail is second growth and contains dense underbrush that is not found on other parts of the trail. From the halfway point to Thrasher Cove the climbs become steeper. At several points there are openings in the forest that may yield excellent views of Port San Juan and the distant Olympic Mountains in Washington.

A good campsite is found about 5 meters (16 feet) off the main trail at its highest point; follow a huge log and an old logging cable. There is room for at least four tents. This campsite has a fine view of the ocean and the Olympic Mountains. The nearest water is about 150 meters (500 feet) away, however, at a stream that may run dry in summer and that lies at the bottom of a steep path. So if you plan to camp at this site, fill your water bottles (and treat or filter that water) at one of the streams after passing the donkey engine.

After the high point, the trail drops steeply to a small stream, called Log Jam Creek, with a bridge across it. After the creek you reach an intersection. Thrasher Cove is to the left down a steep trail with a series of ladders. Face inward when using the ladders and make sure of your footing on the sometimes muddy or slippery rungs. Excellent camping awaits at Thrasher Cove, which has a good water supply from Hobbs Creek.

The trail from Thrasher Cove to 150 Yard Creek can be slow going. At low tides below 1.4 meters (4.6 feet), you can hike along the shore to the west of Thrasher Cove. At first it is slow and tedious travel among slippery, algae-covered boulders, but after you reach the sandstone shelf you can pick up speed. Just before you encounter the sandstone shelf you will have to scramble through a landslide consisting of large boulders. There are some beautiful sea caves to the east of Owen Point, which are well worth exploring if you have the time to do so before high tide. Keep in mind that you must reach the first beach access trail near 150 Yard Creek before the sandstone shelf floods at high tide. The campsite at 150 Yard Creek is small and extremely wet, but it is a useful place to camp if you do not have time to make it to Camper Bay.

A side trail a few minutes past the 150 Yard Creek campsite leads to a rocky shelf at the shoreline. At low tide it is possible to walk along the shelf, but be sure the tide will stay out long enough to allow you to reach the next access point leading to the main trail. One difficulty with hiking along the sandstone shelf is that in several areas sea chasms or surge channels break the shelf. It is usually possible to outflank these by using rough bypass trails. However, it is impossible to use the shelf to reach Camper Bay, so you must regain the trail at the second access trail you meet after 150 Yard Creek. If you have stayed on the trail at 150 Yard Creek, you will likely encounter muddy conditions on the way to Camper Bay. Boardwalks help you over some of the rough sections, but expect to encounter wet conditions in this stretch, since all the mountain runoff collects here. This is the time you will be looking forward to putting on the dry socks in your pack.

Between Trisle Creek and Camper Bay, you will pass through a blowdown area. The trees along the coastal forest protect each other from such blowdowns through wind pruning; because the trees grow evenly, strong ocean winds pass overhead instead of swirling into open spaces. A good example of this pruning can be seen from the

Sandstone shelf, PHOTO BY A. DORST

tidal marker at the beginning of the trail. A wedge of salal growing from the first trees right down to the beach has created a protective belt of vegetation.

There are ladders to be negotiated at Camper Creek. A cable car enables you to get across the creek in high water. If the creek is low, you can wade across; but if you are worried about your ability or the possible danger of high water, you should use the cable car, since Camper Creek can be dangerous to cross. Generally, wading across streams you encounter along the trail is quicker and easier, given the right conditions.

Operating a cable car requires a certain technique. To begin with, each cable car is limited to two individuals. One person should hold the car steady at the platform, while the other one loads the packs in the middle of the car and then gets in the car at one end. The person seated can then hold the car steady while the other person climbs aboard. When all is ready, let go of the line and the car will usually skim quickly along to the middle of the cable. Be careful not to bounce the car or it may disengage from the cable. After you reach the midpoint, the real work begins. Both passengers must exert effort to haul the car to the opposite shore. This task can be quite tedious and tiring, especially on longer cable car crossings. Other cautionary notes: take care not to get your fingers jammed in the pulleys. A good pair of gloves comes in handy for pulling yourself across. If you are traveling in a large group, it is much easier for the members of the group stationed on the platform to haul the car across than it is for the passengers to do so.

Camper Bay is a good campsite with many sites set among beached logs. Like other good sites, however, it tends to become over-crowded during peak season (June to August). It bears repeating that you are in a wilderness area and are directly responsible for the disposal of the waste you create. The cabin at Camper Bay is for the First Nations trail guardians with the Quu'as program. Quu'as is pronounced "co-us" and can be translated as "one people." This group is an amalgamation of the Pacheedaht, Ditidaht and Huu-ay-aht First Nations and provides support services for the operation of the West Coast Trail. Along your hike, you may meet Quu'as trail guardians maintaining and repairing the trail. If you encounter problems with the condition of the trail, such as broken rungs on ladders, report them to the trail guardians or to one of the staff at the trailhead Information Centres.

Between Camper Bay and Sandstone Creek you have a choice of hiking either along the beach or on the trail. The beach route is easier to hike but is only passable when the tide is very low—below 1.2 meters (3.9 feet). At medium tides the shelf will be covered, and even at low tide you may have to wade off the shelf at Sandstone Creek. To regain the main trail at Sandstone, go up the right side of the waterfall using the fixed wire cable. This route is passable only when the stream levels are low, in midsummer. You may have to hike in the stream in several spots. If you are hiking in the opposite direction, look for the beach access trail before you cross the bridge over Sandstone Creek. Hikers going from north to south may have difficulty in climbing onto the shelf at the mouth of Sandstone Creek while carrying a pack. If you are inexperienced or doubtful about the tide, you should probably stay on the trail.

If you elect to hike the trail from Camper Bay, you must first climb the ladders behind the campsite. From the top of the ladders, it is fairly routine slogging to the ladders at Sandstone Creek. The trail from Sandstone Creek to Cullite Creek is relatively easy and can be done quickly. Cullite Cove offers a beautiful campsite on the southeast side of the creek, but the creek gully is usually so wet that it is difficult to maintain a fire. To reach the campsite, do not cross the creek on the cable car but proceed downstream on the east side after you have descended the last of the ladders. The original access trail to the campsite was eliminated in a landslide, so the going may be a bit rough in parts. If you are hiking from the north, you must cross Cullite Creek to gain access to the camping area near the cove.

The trail from Cullite to Logan Creek traverses a large bog. You should stay on the boardwalk, not only to save yourself from taking a mud bath, but also to protect the fragile environment. Most of the plants here are fighting for their survival in the high-acid, low-nitrogen ecosystem.

Once across the bog you face a steep descent by ladders to Logan Creek, which is spanned by an attractive suspension bridge. If you are traveling in a large group, note the precaution that only six people at a time should be on the bridge.

Carmanah Lighthouse, PHOTO BY A. DORST

There is good camping at Logan Creek; if you intend to stop here for the night or for a rest, do not cross the bridge but instead descend the ladders to the campsite. There is good beachcombing at Logan Creek; since it is the most southerly beach along the trail, it collects flotsam from the open ocean. Logan Creek is named after David Logan, a telegraph lineman who was stationed near Clo-oose. Quite the character, he was reported to hike the trail back at the turn of the twentieth century in bare feet. During the wreck of the *Valencia* he played a role in endeavoring to rescue some of the passengers.

Between Logan and Walbran Creeks, you can choose between two routes: slow and muddy but not difficult, and the potentially dangerous beach route, which should be used only when tides are below 2 meters (6.5 feet) and the seas are calm. The tide problem is at Adrenaline Creek, where a deep surge channel runs all the way to a cliff. This channel can be crossed only if the waves are small and the tide is low enough to expose a rock in the middle. Even if this rock is exposed, it is usually slippery, so it is best to slither around the edge of the channel, preferably with the assistance of a rope. The crossing is further complicated by Adrenaline Creek, which plummets from the cliff, making all of the rocks slippery. Inexperienced hikers should not attempt this crossing. It should also not be attempted in the early season (May-June), when the water in Adrenaline Creek is high, since the waterfall tends to prevent the crossing. The PRNPR staff strongly recommend against trying this route. In recent years a number of accidents, including a fatality, have occurred here. A few other surge channels in the area may also present some difficulties.

Walbran Creek is usually crossed via the cable car, but expect a long haul. If you have hiked along the trail, you will descend to the creek on a series of ladders. There is an excellent swimming hole in the creek, but remember to use no soap or only the biodegradable kind if you must bathe. Walbran Creek is named after John T. Walbran, a government steamship captain and the author of *British Columbia Coast Names*.

The Walbran marks the end (or the beginning for hikers traveling from the north) of the difficult hiking. Many groups camp here, and there is a good campsite in the trees on the Port Renfrew side of the creek.

From the Walbran it is only a few hundred meters to a long, sandy beach that is reachable from the creek when the tide is low. Hiking from here to Carmanah along the beach looks easy enough, but the sand is so fine that you must learn a new style of walking. After a while you will discover through experience where the sand is hardest. Try the water's edge or the high-tide mark, where the sand is darker. When the tide is out, the rock shelf provides good hiking. A bypass trail has been built around Vancouver Point, which could be an obstacle at high tide. If you get tired of hiking the beach, there is a good trail from Walbran Creek to Vancouver Point.

Hiking on the beach is the recommended route from Kulaht Creek to Bonilla Creek. A good sheltered campsite is located at Bonilla Creek, just before Bonilla Point. There is also an excellent waterfall nearby if you are in the mood for a shower. The point itself is marked by a large triangle that corresponds to the one across the

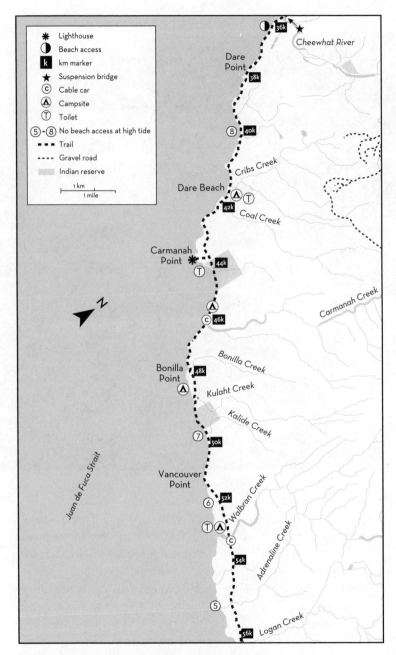

MAP 5: WEST COAST TRAIL—LOGAN CREEK TO CHEEWHAT RIVER

West Coast Trail, PHOTO BY A. DORST

Strait of Juan de Fuca at Cape Flattery; these signs mark the official designation of the strait as internal waters, as opposed to the open ocean. Bonilla means "high" in Spanish. Originally Bonilla Point was assigned as a name for Carmanah Point to the northwest, where the lighthouse stands atop the cliff. By mistake the name was given to the present point, which is low and belies its Spanish name.

Carmanah Creek may be crossed by wading or by using the cable car. If you wade across, use a staff or pole for balance. You should not try to wade across this creek in high water or on an incoming tide. There is good camping on the Bamfield side of Carmanah Creek, but many other parts of wide, sweeping Carmanah Beach are clogged with driftwood. At the Bamfield end of the beach on the Indian reserve is a small settlement. Over the past few years the Nytom family has operated a small restaurant and food store here. The beer is cold and the conversation as spicy as the food.

At the end of Carmanah Beach, you will spy a trail opening between some alder that leads to a ladder. The trail climbs over the headland behind Carmanah lighthouse and through the forest to the next beach. The lighthouse has been here since 1891. It is possible to hike around Carmanah Point at low tide, but expect to do a fair amount of scrambling on slippery rocks. The section from Carmanah Point to Klanawa River is, in the opinion of many hikers, the most scenic part of the trail. Not only does the terrain alternate between forest and coastline, but the cliffs are less continuous, offering more opportunity for beach exploration.

At the Bay of the Cribs, the hiking is easy by either beach or forest. A prominent headland dominates the south end of the bay, visible almost to Nitinat Narrows. You may continue along the shelves from here to Dare Point, but only at low tide. A surge channel along the way may prove difficult to negotiate. If the tide is too high, use the access trails and ladders located both before and after this chasm. The trail from the Cribs rises steeply and traverses the top of the cliff almost to Dare Point, where it drops to sea level. After descending the long flight of stairs, hikers may regain the beach near Dare Point at the end of the boardwalk. A campsite with water is located at the south end of the sandy beach.

From Dare Point to the Cheewhat River the trail goes over old sand dunes that have been colonized by forest. There are many flat, sheltered campsites along the trail as well as camping spots along the beach. Drinking water can be difficult to find; the nearest places to fill your water bottles are the north side of the Cheewhat Bridge and the south end of the sandy beach.

The Cheewhat is a slow-flowing tidal river called "river of urine" by the Ditidaht because of its color and bad taste. Better drinking water is available from a small creek located just off the trail past the north end of the bridge. The bridge across the Cheewhat was built in 1976 and is a favorite subject of photographers. If you are hiking to Port Renfrew, keep to the right after crossing the bridge. Cheewhat Lake is located approximately 5 kilometers (3 miles) north of this spot but is not reachable by trail. The lake is a wintering ground for rare trumpeter swans.

The area around Clo-oose has many signs of past settlement. White settlers began to arrive in the 1880s when William Grove obtained an acre of land before the boundaries of the Indian reserve were established in 1892. In the 1890s William Stone arrived as the first missionary in the area, and the Logan family came to homestead. In 1912, land was developed, and several dozen white people settled in the area, mainly to the east and west of Clo-oose. At one time there was a proposal for a large village to be hewn out of the wilderness here. The proponents of this scheme did not like the name Clo-oose and petitioned the B.C. government to change the name to Clovelly. The building scheme failed when the passengers on the steamer from Victoria that was hired to bring prospective purchasers to the area were not able to disembark due to high seas.

Clo-oose residents, along with the lighthouse keepers and the linemen, often played heroic roles in the rescue of shipwrecked mariners. This small community contributed a disproportionate share of young men to military service in World War I, and after the war the community declined. Other factors were isolation, the closing of the fish cannery on Nitinat Lake, the decline of the salmon fishery and, in the 1950s, the withdrawal of the coastal steamer *Maquinna* as many west coast communities became accessible by road or float plane. The last of the original white families left in 1952. With the creation of the national park, the private land holdings were all expropriated and transferred to the federal government.

Hikers are required by the Ditidaht Band to remain on the trail through the Clo-oose area. Quu'as guardians patrol the trail and all reserve lands, which are off-limits for camping and exploring. All such lands are well marked with signs advising hikers that there is no trespassing or camping on reserve land.

From Clo-oose, the trail climbs to the top of a cliff, where there are spectacular views, especially at sunset. Watch your footing here,

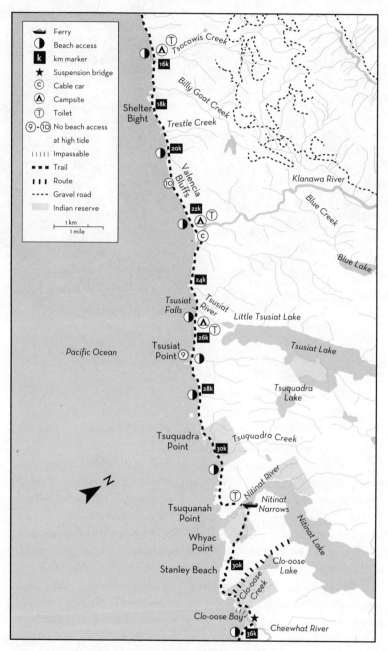

Legend:
- Ferry
- Beach access
- k — km marker
- ★ — Suspension bridge
- © — Cable car
- Ⓐ — Campsite
- Ⓣ — Toilet
- ⑨-⑩ — No beach access at high tide
- ||||| — Impassable
- ▪▪▪ — Trail
- ▮▮▮ — Route
- --- — Gravel road
- Indian reserve

1 km
1 mile

Tsocowis Creek
16k
18k
Shelter Bight
Billy Goat Creek
Trestle Creek
20k
Valencia Bluffs
⑩
Klanawa River
Blue Creek
22k
©
Blue Lake
24k
Tsusiat Falls
Tsusiat River
Little Tsusiat Lake
26k
Tsusiat Point ⑨
Tsusiat Lake
Pacific Ocean
28k
Tsuquadra Lake
Tsuquadra Point
30k
Tsuquadra Creek
Nitinat River
Ⓣ
Nitinat Narrows
Tsuquanah Point
Nitinat Lake
Whyac Point
Stanley Beach
30k
Clo-oose Lake
Clo-oose Creek
Clo-oose Bay ★
Cheewhat River
36k

MAP 6: WEST COAST TRAIL—CHEEWHAT RIVER TO TSOCOWIS CREEK

Tsusiat Falls, PHOTO BY A. DORST

since the drop-off is quite steep. It is not possible to hike along the shore all the way from Clo-oose to Whyac.

Whyac is a very old village, possibly one of the oldest on the west coast of North America. When the first white explorer, Dr. Robert Brown, traveled to this area in 1864, Whyac was the principal village of the Ditidaht people. It was strongly fortified and considered to be impregnable by the inhabitants. Dr. Brown described the Ditidaht as having "a high reputation as hunters, whale fishers, and warriors."

The trail bypasses Whyac, and you must remain on the trail and not visit the village. In the past, hikers have been responsible for vandalizing and destroying many sacred sites of the First Nations people.

At Nitinat Narrows there is a ferry service to take you across; you paid the fees for the crossing in advance when Parks Canada collected your permit fees. The operator is stationed on the south side of the narrows at the small dock. If you are hiking from the north, you may have to wait until you are spotted. During the summer the operator may have cold drinks and fresh crab for sale. If you wish, you may hire a boat to take you out from the trail down the length of Nitinat Lake to Ditidaht Village, at the end of the lake. The cost of this trip is $25 per person at the time of this publication.

Nitinat Narrows is one of the most spectacular locations on the entire west coast of Vancouver Island and also one of the most dangerous. Tidal currents roar through at speeds up to 8 knots, creating treacherous whirlpools. The outgoing tide is particularly dangerous—as it meets incoming ocean swells, huge standing waves are formed. Many drownings have occurred here. Do not try to swim across this channel, even if you are stranded and waiting for a ferry to arrive.

The portion of the trail between Nitinat Narrows and the Klanawa River is considered by many to be the most dramatically beautiful part of the West Coast Trail. It has almost everything: sweeping sandy beaches, sea caves, rocky headlands, shelves teeming with marine life and the famous Tsusiat Falls. It can be hiked in a long day but deserves a more leisurely visit.

From the narrows the trail climbs again, and you get glimpses of the sea as it surges against headlands and chasms. Between here and Tsusiat Falls there are many camping areas, but water can be a problem during the dry season. The trail rejoins the beach about 1.5 kilometers (about 1 mile) from Nitinat, and from this point to Tsusiat Falls you can do most of your hiking along the beach. You will have to leave the beach route to get around the headlands at Tsuquadra Point and Tsusiat Point, the location of Hole-in-the-Wall, and certain other parts are passable only if the tide is right. There is no trespassing at the Tsuquadra Indian reserve. This area is patrolled by Quu'as guardians, who are stationed at a cabin near Tsuquadra Creek.

Tsusiat Falls has become a popular gathering place; during the height of the season, many groups will be camped here. Consequently, litter and sanitation are problems. In particular, the shallow sea caves in the Tsusiat area should not be used as latrines. You should carry a small trowel or other digging tool in order to properly dispose of your waste in the forest floor. The outhouse is located towards the north end of the beach past the falls, in the trees near the cliff. There are also caches for storage of food nearby. You should follow the instructions for use of these devices. Parks Canada has supplied outhouses and food caches at most of the major camping sites along the trail to help remedy problems with human waste disposal as well as to protect food supplies from wild critters.

From Tsusiat Falls to the Klanawa River, you are completely separated from the ocean except for one or two rough and steep access points. The cable car ride across the Klanawa is an exciting experience, but if you are alone, the journey will be hard on your shoulders. It is best if one person rides in the car and pulls while a partner assists from shore. The Klanawa, like the Cheewhat, is tidal, so you may have to go a fair way upstream to obtain potable water. You should also keep the tide in mind when selecting your picturesque campsite on the banks of the river.

It is possible to hike from the Klanawa to the trail's end in one day, but it is a long hike and the scenery deserves to be enjoyed. Water is plentiful, with the possible exception of the first 4 kilometers (2.5 miles) west of the Klanawa River. The trail proceeds mainly through the forest, but there are various spots where the beach is accessible for extended walking. You can trek from the Klanawa to Michigan Creek on the beach, except for the section between Trestle Creek and Tsocowis Creek.

The famous *Valencia* wreck of 1906 occurred near Shelter Bight, about 4 kilometers (2.5 miles) west of the mouth of the Klanawa River. An overview of the wreck site appears where the trail skirts the cliffs through an old burn, just west of a donkey engine that was left by trail builders in 1909. Over the years, the *Valencia* has sunk completely, and no remnants of wreckage are visible.

The capstan on the rocks near Shelter Bight may have come from the four-masted steam schooner *Robert E. Lewers*, which went aground in 1923. In 1895, the magnificent iron square-rigger *Janet Cowan* was wrecked near here, and its remains are still visible in a surge channel at the outlet of Billy Goat Creek. Finally, at the mouth of Michigan Creek lie the boiler and some smaller parts of the steam schooner *Michigan*, wrecked in 1893.

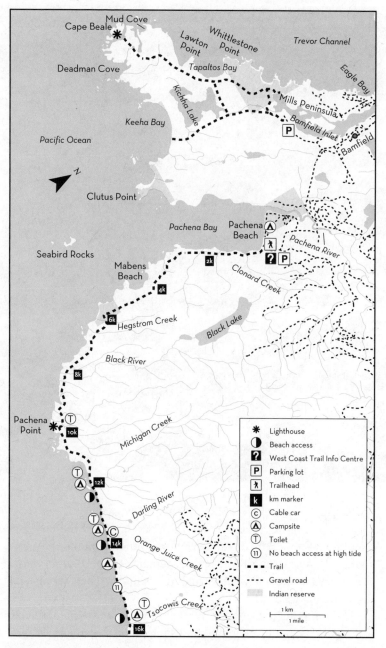

MAP 7: WEST COAST TRAIL—TSOCOWIS CREEK TO PACHENA BAY

Rocky headland, PHOTO BY A. DORST

The Darling River can be forded by wading, and the crossing should pose little difficulty under normal runoff conditions. At the mouth of the Darling River are the remains of the *Uzbekistan*, a Russian steamship that went down in 1943 while carrying war materials from the west coast.

The campsites at Darling River, being fairly close to the Pachena Bay trailhead, are heavily used and susceptible to damage. Hikers are urged to treat the area gently and in particular to build fires only on the beach. Additional camping can be found near Tsocowis Creek and Michigan Creek. An especially good campsite replete with small but dry caves is located near Orange Juice Creek, the small creek to the east of the Darling River. Campers at either Michigan Creek or Darling River will have difficulty finding kindling for a fire.

From Michigan Creek the trail climbs up through the forest to the Pachena lighthouse. At the time of publication, the lighthouse at Pachena Point is staffed and drinking water is available on the grounds.

The trail from Pachena Point to the trailhead is almost a road; for many years it was the supply road for the lighthouse. The many gullies make it harder to hike than one would expect, and the trail itself is almost entirely in the forest, with few viewpoints. You may want to try one or more of the several water access or view paths. In fall and early spring, sea lions can be spotted on Flat Rocks, just offshore.

Just beyond the trail's end is an Information Centre staffed by PRNPR employees and open from 9:00 a.m. to 5:00 p.m. daily from May 1 until October 1. You must drop off your West Coast Trail permit at the Information Centre.

To reach Bamfield, you must go through the parking lot to the main road; it is a dusty, 5-kilometer walk into town. Bamfield has accommodations and supplies and is also the terminus for the Bamfield–Port Alberni ferry, the MV *Lady Rose*.

If you want to camp at Pachena Bay, note that most of the beach area lies within a reserve. The Huu-ay-aht First Nation, which owns the reserve, operates a commercial campground. Camping is also permitted on the beach near the end of the trail for a maximum stay of three nights. Camping is not permitted on the grassy area adjacent to the Information Centre.

> ## HIKING AROUND BAMFIELD

If you have to wait in Bamfield a day or two for transportation out or are simply exploring the area, there are a few day hikes and short excursions worth taking. A visit to the original town site of Bamfield on the west side of Bamfield Inlet is recommended. Getting across the inlet should not be much of a problem, since water taxis regularly go back and forth. Just ask at the main dock.

The original townsite of Bamfield is much more interesting than the east side. Very few cars are seen here, and a maze of walking trails connects with the "main street"—a boardwalk along the waterfront. Short jaunts can be made to Brady Beach and other beaches beyond by following the occasional sign.

Hiking to Cape Beale starts at a well-marked trailhead at the end of Imperial Eagle Road on the east side of the inlet, about half a kilometer before the government wharf. There is limited parking about 40 meters (130 feet) up the road from the trailhead. No parking is permitted at the trailhead itself. To reach Cape Beale, proceed along the trail in a southerly direction until you reach Kichha Lake. At the junction take the right branch west to Tapaltos Bay. When you reach Tapaltos Bay, hike along the beach for about two-thirds of its length to a point where the trail enters the forest. The rest of the trail can be difficult as a result of mud and broken boardwalks. If your goal is the Cape Beale lighthouse, you must reach the final channel at low tide, which is the only time when it is dry. There is no camping at the lighthouse, so don't get stranded by the incoming tide.

Another interesting side trip takes you to Keeha Bay. At the Y junction at the northern tip of Kichha Lake, take the trail to your left, which follows the east side of the lake. The trail is in rough condition towards the southern end of the lake; you may have to bushwhack or slog through mud to reach dry, high ground. Cape Beale or Pachena Bay may be reached from Keeha Bay, but you have to scramble over rocks, do some grueling bushwhacking and wait for low tides in certain stretches to get around otherwise impassable headlands.

4

CARMANAH WALBRAN
PROVINCIAL PARK

· · · · ·

> AVERAGE RATING: 2 C

> ACCESS: Highway 18 from Duncan to Lake Cowichan, then logging roads

> HAZARDS: Creek crossings, route-finding in parts, portions of trail not maintained

> SPECIAL FEATURES: Giant trees, beautiful pools, old-growth forests, waterfalls, pristine lakes

> MAPS 1:20,000: 92C057 (Vancouver Point) · 92C067 (Carmanah Point) · 92C068 (House Cone) · 92C077 (Doobah Lake)
1:50,000: 92C10 (Carmanah Creek)
A useful map showing access and trail routes is the *South and Central Vancouver Island Recreation Map* produced by the Carmanah Forestry Society, which is available at outdoor stores or retail map stores.

> TIDE TABLES: Not required

> *Mid-Carmanah trailhead to Paradise Pool*
DISTANCE: 6.5 km (4 miles) (one way) · TIME: 2.5–3 hours
RATING: 2 C
Trail is easy at first, then gets progressively rougher

> *West Walbran trailhead near Fletcher Falls to Haddon-1000*
DISTANCE: 7.5 km (4.7 miles) (one way) · TIME: 3–4 hours
RATING: 2 D
Some tricky log crossings. Not maintained by BC Parks

> *Central Walbran Trail from trailhead near Botley Lake to West Walbran Trail*
DISTANCE: 4 km (2.5 miles) (one way) · TIME: 2–3 hours · RATING: 2 D
For experienced hikers only. Not maintained by BC Parks

> ACCESS AND PERMITS
At present there are no public transportation services to Carmanah Walbran Provincial Park. You will need a vehicle with good tires and traction as well as high clearance to reach any of the hiking trails in this area. To reach the middle of the Carmanah Valley, where you will find a campground as well as the majority of the large trees, follow the logging roads along Cowichan Lake to Nitinat Lake. You may take either the route around the northern side of Cowichan Lake through Youbou or along the southern side through Honeymoon Bay and Caycuse to get to Nitinat Lake. Follow the signs for Carmanah Walbran Provincial Park. Drive past the turnoff to Ditidaht Village at Nitinat Lake and continue along South Mainline until you reach the Caycuse River Bridge. You may encounter a safety checkpoint here. You should stop for information and to obtain the operator's instructions. The operator is in radio contact with logging trucks in the vicinity and will advise the drivers of your presence. Turn right after crossing the bridge and go along Rosander Mainline logging road for about 30 kilometers (19 miles). The road will climb steadily as you skirt Nitinat Lake before heading down and turning left for the Carmanah Valley.

Gravel bar, Carmanah Creek

There is a large parking lot at the end of the road. The trail system is well marked. If you plan on camping here, there are a few campsites and pit toilets located along the old road that proceeds east from the parking lot.

Access to the Walbran Valley is a little more complicated. It is a good idea to pick up a map of logging roads of southwest Vancouver Island or purchase the map produced by the Carmanah Forestry Society to assist you in finding the various trailheads. Check out their Web site, www.carmanah.ca, and click on the icon for Access Maps.

To reach the main trail system of the Walbran, follow the south side of Cowichan Lake past Honeymoon Bay. Just past Caycuse Camp, an old forestry camp, turn left along Caycuse Mainline (also called Nixon Creek Mainline) until you reach a junction with McClure Lake Mainline, and continue along this road until you reach McClure Lake. At the junction at the end of the lake, take the left fork onto Walbran Mainline and continue for several kilometers until you reach Glad Lake West. Turn right and cross a bridge over the western branch of Walbran Creek. Continue up the hill and then descend to cross the main stem of the Walbran. The West Walbran Trail starts near the bridge.

To get to the Central Walbran trailhead near Botley Lake, follow the instructions above until you reach the Y junction at the end of McClure Lake. Take the left fork onto Walbran Mainline and follow it for 2 kilometers (a little more than a mile) to another Y junction. The right fork leads down to Botley Lake. Keep to the left at any intersection. At this writing, the road is in poor condition, so exercise caution when traveling along it.

For the West Walbran trailhead, follow the above instructions for Walbran Mainline but keep to the right at the second Y junction. (The left fork descends to Botley Lake.) Turn left onto Haddon Mainline, go past Hadican Lake on your right and continue for 5 kilometers (3 miles) until you cross a narrow bridge. Continue straight ahead to a Y junction, where you will take the right fork which is Haddon-1000. This road is overgrown with alder at time of publication but it is passable. You will find the trailhead and a small place to park your vehicle at the end of the road.

A backcountry camping fee is charged at Carmanah Walbran Provincial Park; self-registration vaults are located in the parking lot at the Carmanah Valley trailhead. The current fee is $5 per person per day. There are no self-registration vaults for permits for camping in the Walbran portion of the park.

> ## TRAIL DESCRIPTIONS AND HISTORY

Carmanah Walbran Provincial Park is well worth visiting. Although strictly speaking the trails in this park are not coastal trails, they do afford access to some of the most beautiful old-growth forests left on the west coast. Large Sitka spruce and hemlock as well as ancient western red cedars line the clear, rushing waters and deep aquamarine pools of Carmanah and Walbran creeks. Unlike the coastal trails, which resound with the omnipresent sound of crashing surf, the trails in this park will impress you with their silence.

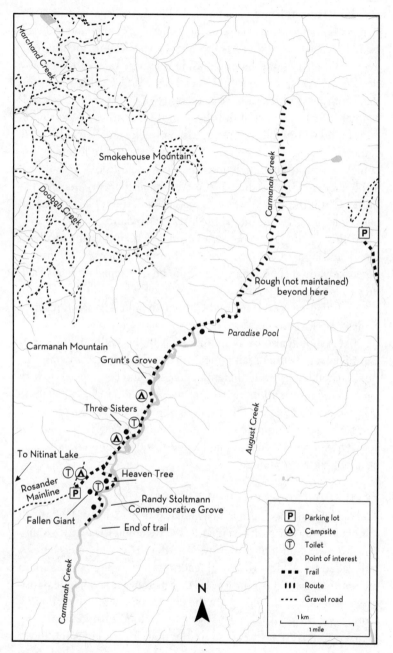

Marchand Creek

Doobah Creek

Smokehouse Mountain

Carmanah Creek

P

Rough (not maintained)
beyond here

Paradise Pool

Carmanah Mountain

Grunt's Grove

Three Sisters

August Creek

To Nitinat Lake

Rosander
Mainline

Heaven Tree

Randy Stoltmann
Commemorative Grove

Fallen Giant

End of trail

Carmanah Creek

N

P	Parking lot
A	Campsite
T	Toilet
●	Point of interest
▪▪▪	Trail
|||	Route
----	Gravel road

1 km
1 mile

MAP 8: CARMANAH VALLEY

The lower and mid-Carmanah Valley became a park in 1991. Large adjoining tracts of land in the upper Carmanah and the Walbran Creek system were added to the park by the province in 1995. The result of this land being set aside is a large reserve adjacent to the West Coast Trail that preserves Logan and Cullite Creeks in their entirety as well as a large percentage of Carmanah Creek. It is estimated that 2 percent of British Columbia's coastal old-growth forest is found within the confines of this park. The creation of this park came about after much controversy, disputes with the logging companies that controlled the tenure and mass protests followed by civil disobedience. Groups such as the Carmanah Forestry Society, the Sierra Club and the Western Canada Wilderness Committee all worked to preserve this incredible forest as parkland.

At this writing BC Parks is discouraging hiking in the Walbran Creek and upper Carmanah Creek portions of the park because of potentially unsafe conditions. There are no developed BC Parks facilities or trails in the Walbran Valley. The only area in the park with well-maintained trails is the mid-Carmanah Valley, which is reached via Rosander Mainline.

Hikers should also be aware that trails in the Walbran and upper Carmanah are neither maintained nor patrolled by BC Parks rangers. Be prepared to encounter potential dangers, and be prepared to turn back. The information listed in this guide may be inaccurate because of changing conditions along the trail. Be sure to let others know of your hiking plans, and do not take unnecessary risks. No active rescue services are available, and if you are injured, help may be a long time in coming.

> ### TRAILS IN THE CARMANAH VALLEY

The one area of the Carmanah Walbran Provincial Park that is well maintained is near park headquarters at the end of Rosander Mainline. You will find tent platforms, drinking water and toilets here. A trail called the Valley Mist Trail leads down from the parking lot to the home of giant Sitka spruce. Since Sitka spruce has fragile, sensitive roots, you should remain on the planks so as not to erode the soil around the trees. After a 1.3-kilometer (0.8-mile) hike along the planked trail, you will reach a T junction. To the right the lower

Carmanah Trail continues downstream to Heaven Tree, the Fallen Giant and the Randy Stoltmann Commemorative Grove (formerly known as Heaven's Grove). This grove is named for the B.C. conservationist who was instrumental in convincing many people and the provincial government that this area was worth preserving from the logger's saw. An information board in this area provides details about his life. The lower trail is closed approximately 500 meters (550 yards) past this grove. The trail used to continue downstream to visit the Carmanah Giant and to join the West Coast Trail, but the lower trail has been closed by BC Parks due to its extremely unsafe condition. Access to the West Coast Trail from Carmanah Walbran Provincial Park is not permitted.

If you turn left at the T junction, you will hike upstream along the middle Carmanah Trail and encounter the Three Sisters, a group of three very tall spruce, after a hike of 1.2 kilometers (0.75 mile). No camping is permitted south of this grove. Beyond the Three Sisters, the trail becomes rougher. The first wilderness campsite, Grunt's Grove, is located about another 2 kilometers (about a mile) north of here in a grove of spruce just off the trail. There are some additional campsites along the gravel streambed during the summer, when the water levels have dropped. All of the campsites of Carmanah Walbran are wilderness sites. Wilderness camping means no-trace camping and thus no campfires. The trail meanders away from the creek for another 2 kilometers (about a mile) and returns to the stream, where there is an excellent wilderness campsite near Paradise Pool, a deep, emerald-green pool that is perfect for bathing in hot weather.

The trail past this point has been officially closed by BC Parks, is not maintained and is better described as a route rather than a trail. The bridge across the small gorge at the headwaters of Carmanah Creek is in a dangerous state. Since BC Parks has no intention of fixing it, it is not recommended that the upper Carmanah be used for hiking.

The following instructions are for travelers who do wish to explore the upper Carmanah Basin. From Paradise Pool, the route crosses Carmanah Creek to the east side on a log bridge. This creek crossing may be treacherous in high water. The trail on the east side tends to be wet for the first few kilometers. After a hike of 1 kilometer (0.6 mile) you will reach Mystic's Hollow Camp, on a wide gravel bench beside Carmanah Creek. The large tributary that enters Carmanah Creek just north of here is August Creek. The creek crossing at August Creek can also be difficult to negotiate over a logjam.

The Upper Valley Trail continues along the east side of Carmanah Creek for another 7.5 kilometers (4.6 miles) to the Headwaters trailhead. Here you will encounter rougher going than in the mid-Carmanah but also substantially fewer hikers. After August Creek the upper trail ascends to benchland away from the creek for the next few kilometers. The path then descends to a good campsite at Sleepy Hollow beside Maxine Creek, a clear tributary of the Carmanah. As the trail traverses the sloping side hills, it crosses a blow-down area of windfallen hemlock. After the blowdown, the path rejoins the creek, where there is a beautiful box canyon followed by pools and cascades. Camp Patience is just beyond this point. The Headwaters trailhead is only 3.3 kilometers (2 miles) from here.

The trail ascends to another series of loud waterfalls that resound through the quiet forest. For many years the Western Canada Wilderness Committee (WCWC) conducted research into the canopy life in this area; the organization discovered several marbled murrelet nests here. The WCWC also operated a research camp called Hummingbird Camp in a flat area beside the creek about half a kilometer (a third of a mile) before the end of the upper trail. The bridge that spans the gorge near the trailhead is in a dangerous state. Just before the bridge you will encounter a planked trail with the names of some of the trail builders carved into the planks.

> ### TRAILS IN THE WALBRAN VALLEY

There are two main trail systems in the Walbran Valley: the West Walbran Trail and the Central Walbran Trail. None of the trails are maintained by BC Parks. All trails were built by volunteers of the Carmanah Forestry Society in an attempt to promote the area before it was logged. The trailhead to the West Walbran is near the logging bridge over the main stem of Walbran Creek. Look for the start in the wooded area to the right of the bridge after you cross it. Parking is available off the logging road that continues to the left. An alternative

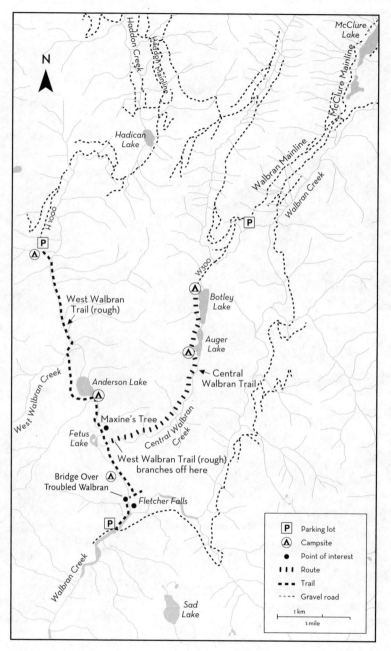

N

McClure
Lake

Haddon Creek

Haddon Mainline

McClure Mainline

Hadican
Lake

Walbran Mainline

Walbran Creek

H1000

P
Ⓐ

West Walbran
Trail (rough)

W300

P

Ⓐ Botley
Lake

Ⓐ Auger
Lake

← Central
Walbran Trail

West Walbran Creek

Anderson Lake

Ⓐ

Maxine's Tree

Fetus
Lake

Central Walbran Creek

West Walbran Trail (rough)
branches off here

Bridge Over
Troubled Walbran

Ⓐ

Fletcher Falls

P

Walbran Creek

Sad
Lake

P	Parking lot
Ⓐ	Campsite
●	Point of interest
┇ ┇ ┇	Route
▬ ▬ ▬	Trail
- - - -	Gravel road

1 km

1 mile

MAP 9: WALBRAN VALLEY

Nurse log

approach to starting the trail is to cross the bridge and follow the logging road to the left and then to the right up a clear-cut slope as it
switchbacks. A trail leads into the forest near the end of this spur road.
The clear-cut area is not included within the park.

The West Walbran Trail ascends alongside Fletcher Falls. There
are some side trails that give good views of the falls. A short distance
past the falls, you will reach a floating bridge, the "bridge over the
troubled Walbran," which gains access to the east side of the creek.
When you complete the crossing, the West Walbran Trail leads left
in a northerly direction. If you turn to the right, you will hike for
about 20 minutes to a huge western red cedar and Castle Grove.

The West Walbran Trail enters the park a few hundred meters
after the floating bridge. The trail is in rough shape in places and
you can expect to encounter mud and many roots criss-crossing the
trail. The first wilderness campsite is Giggling Spruce, in a small
grove of large Sitka beside the creek. After a few kilometers of slogging you will cross the Central Walbran Creek, which is also called
Botley Creek. There is no bridge crossing here, and you may have to
wade the creek, depending on the amount of water flowing through.
A short distance past this creek crossing, you will reach a junction
with the Central Walbran Trail that leads to Auger Lake and Botley
Lake. If you continue along the West Walbran Trail, you will catch
glimpses of Fetus Lake, a shallow, marshy body of water to the west.
One of the main attractions along the West Walbran Trail is Maxine's Tree, an enormous Sitka spruce named for the daughter of Syd
Haskell, the founder of the Carmanah Forestry Society; he helped
organize many of the volunteers who built the trails in this area.

The trail recrosses Walbran Creek to the west side shortly past
Maxine's Tree and continues up to Anderson Lake. There is a good
campsite on the gravel at the south end of the lake adjacent to a tributary. The trail past the lake tends to be a bit confusing, and you may
lose it. Basically, the path follows the west side of the lake, although
you will be hiking away from the lake for most of the trip. At the
head of Anderson Lake, the trail descends through a marshy area
and meets a side stream. This stream may have to be waded in high
water. The trail then crosses West Walbran Creek on a tricky log
crossing to the east side. From this point, the route follows the creek

Anderson Lake, Walbran Valley

through marsh, thicket and spruce forest. One final creek crossing awaits you near the trailhead; an easily crossed log will take you to the west side. Camp Perfection is found here nestled among the old growth.

The trailhead for the Central Walbran Trail is reached via McClure Lake Mainline and Walbran Mainline. Since the spur logging road off Walbran Mainline is rough, you may have to hike in the 2.5 kilometers (1.5 miles) to the trailhead. The trail crosses a small stream and reaches the shore of Botley Lake a few minutes from the trailhead. The path wends its way past Botley Lake to Auger Lake. Midway down Auger Lake there is a grove of large western cedars. The trail dissipates to a rougher route after Auger Lake, and the experienced hiker will be able to reach its junction with the West Walbran Trail as outlined above.

It bears repeating that none of the trails in the Walbran Valley are maintained. You may encounter washouts and detours around fallen trees. It is easy to lose the trail in many sections. Thus, hiking in the Walbran is not recommended for novices.

5

LONG BEACH AND THE
TOFINO/UCLUELET AREA

· · · · ·

> **AVERAGE RATING:** 2 B I (10 trails)

> **ACCESS:** Highway 4 and the Pacific Rim Highway (from Port
Alberni). Island Coach Lines or Tofino Bus (from Victoria,
Nanaimo or Port Alberni). Air service to Tofino includes Regency
Express (from Vancouver) and Global Charters (from Victoria).
Water taxis for trails beyond Tofino.

> **HAZARDS:** Tides, rogue waves, creek and log crossings, restricted
beach access in spots

> **SPECIAL FEATURES:** Lighthouse, ocean views, signed First
Nations heritage sites, hot springs, beach walks, tide pools, bird
watching, wildlife

> **MAPS 1:20,000:** 092C092 (Florencia Bay) · 092C093 (Ucluelet)
092F001 (Gowlland Rocks) · 092F002 (Long Beach) · 092F011
(Wickaninnish Island)
1:50,000: 92C13 (Ucluelet) · 92F04 (Tofino)
A 1:75,000 map entitled *Backroad Map and Outdoor Recreation
Guide to Tofino, Ucluelet and Pacific Rim Area* is available commercially from Pacific Rim Informative Adventures Ltd., Ucluelet.

> **TIDE TABLES:** Zone 11. For hikes around Ucluelet, use Ucluelet
tide tables. Use Tofino tables for hikes near there.

Amphitrite Lighthouse

> **SECTIONS AT A GLANCE** appear with the individual hikes.

> **ACCESS AND PERMITS**
Access by vehicle to hikes in the Long Beach and Tofino/Ucluelet area is by far the easiest to arrange of all the hikes listed in this book. Take Highway 4 from Port Alberni and travel along the paved but winding road until you reach its terminus at the T intersection with the Pacific Rim Highway. If you turn left here you will arrive at Ucluelet; a right-hand turn leads to Tofino. All of the trails listed in this section are accessible from the Pacific Rim Highway or from Tofino.

There are public transportation facilities to get you to the beach. Island Coach Lines is a bus service that operates between Tofino and Victoria through Nanaimo and Port Alberni. Phone toll-free 1-800-318-0818 for schedules and information. At this time there is another bus service, the Tofino Bus, that runs from Victoria and Nanaimo to the Long Beach area. It stops off at some of the trailheads listed in this chapter. For schedules and fares, phone toll free 1-866-986-3466 or go to their Web site at www.tofinobus.com. They also operate the Beach Bus that runs between Tofino and Ucluelet, with stops in between.

There is an airport at Tofino, and Regency Express has daily flights from Vancouver South Terminal to Tofino. Phone toll-free 1-800-228-6608 for further information. Flights between Victoria and Tofino are handled by Global Charters, who can be reached toll-free at 1-866-656-4132.

For the trails located within Pacific Rim National Park Reserve, you will have to pay a park user fee during the summer season (mid-March to mid-October). This fee is payable at machines located at most major parking lots in the park.

If you are planning on staying and hiking in the national park area for a few days, this table sets out the current fees.

> ENTRY: Parking, in lieu of entry

Per vehicle, per day $10.00

Per vehicle, annual $45.00

Per vehicle, annual senior (over 65) $38.25

Late payment $35.00

> CAMPING: 1 night

Long Beach (Green Point)—semi-serviced site (drive-in) with toilets $20.00

Long Beach (Green Point)—primitive site (walk-in) $14.00

For trails beyond Tofino, water taxis are available to Vargas and Flores islands as well as Hot Springs Cove. The *Ahousaht Pride* makes daily trips of approximately 45 minutes' duration to and from Ahousat, on Flores Island. It leaves Ahousat at 8:00 a.m. for Tofino, then departs from the First Street Dock in Tofino at 10:30 a.m. It then leaves Ahousat at 1:00 p.m. and returns from Tofino at 4:00 p.m.

Cost is $14 per person one-way. Tell the crew or captain where you are headed (e.g., Wild Side Trail or Hummingbird Hostel), and you will be dropped off at the correct dock. The fee for hiking the Wild Side Trail is a suggested donation of $20 per person.

Cougar Island Water Taxi also runs between Ahousat and Tofino, but does not operate on a fixed schedule although it functions very much like a regular taxi service. They will travel when they get enough passengers to warrant their making the trip. They can usually be reached by radio phone on channels 68 through 72. If you are stuck in Ahousat and need to get back to Tofino, ask for assistance at the Maaktusiis General Store above the hydro dock. A number of tour operators also have daily excursions to Flores or Vargas islands, which may include beach drop-off and pickup.

For more information on the Wild Side Trail or access, call the Ahousaht Band office at 250-670-9531. Or phone the Wild Side Trail phone number: 250-670-9586. The e-mail address is walk-thewildside@alberni.net. During the peak season in 2004, Clayoquot Sound Adventures offered drop-off service at the trailhead at Cow Bay and pickup at Ahousat. It is not known if this service will continue into the 2005 season. Phone 250-725-2521 for further information.

> **TRAIL DESCRIPTIONS AND HISTORY**

Unlike many of the other trails described in this book, the trails in the Ucluelet and Tofino area are shorter day hikes rather than multiday backpacking treks. Generally the trails are not only shorter but considerably easier to hike, and better maintained than the longer trails. Some of these trails may be done in a few hours and others may take a long day. Numerous facilities for dining and accommodation are available in either of the two main towns on the Long Beach Peninsula. Hiking these trails in conjunction with a weekend or longer stay allows the visitor to experience the beauty of the west coast in an easily accessible fashion. However, the same hazards, such as tides, rogue waves, weather and hypothermia, that apply to the longer trails must be considered if you intend to walk these trails. The hikes are described in this chapter from south to north, going from Ucluelet to Tofino.

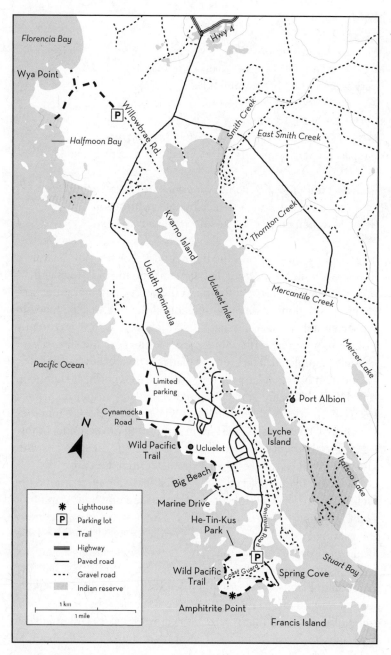

Florencia Bay

Wya Point

Hwy 4

🅿

Willowbrae Rd.

— *Halfmoon Bay*

Smith Creek

East Smith Creek

Kvarno Island

Ucluelet Inlet

Thornton Creek

Ucluth Peninsula

Mercantile Creek

Pacific Ocean

Mercer Lake

Limited parking

Port Albion

Cynamocka Road

Wild Pacific Trail

● Ucluelet

Lyche Island

Iqtsoo Lake

Big Beach

Marine Drive

Peninsula Road

He-Tin-Kus Park

Stuart Bay

N

Wild Pacific Trail

🅿

Coast Guard

Spring Cove

Amphitrite Point

Francis Island

✳	Lighthouse
🅿	Parking lot
– – –	Trail
≡	Highway
——	Paved road
····	Gravel road
▒	Indian reserve

1 km

1 mile

MAP 10: WILD PACIFIC TRAIL

Wild Pacific Trail
> **SECTIONS AT A GLANCE**
> *Phase 1, Ucluth Peninsula*
2.5 km (1.5 miles) one way · TIME: 1.5 hours · RATING: 2 A
Very scenic—highly recommended

> *Phase 2, km 2.5 to marker 4*
1.5 km (1 mile) one way · TIME: 30 minutes · RATING: 1 A
On pavement or gravel shoulder of road—not recommended

> *Phases 3 and 4, Big Beach to junction with bike path at km 8.5*
4 km (2.5 miles) one way · TIME: 2 hours · RATING: 2 B
Some elevation changes. Take bike path back to Ucluelet

The Wild Pacific Trail was the brainchild of "Oyster Jim" Martin, a long-time resident of Ucluelet. Its construction was financed by funds donated to the Wild Pacific Trail Society, a non-profit organization. (Donations towards completion of the trail may be made to the society at Box 572, Ucluelet, B.C. V0R 3A0.) The trail is currently a work-in-progress, with some portions close to the townsite of Ucluelet completed. The eventual plan is to link up this trail with the Pacific Rim National Park Reserve farther to the north, at Halfmoon Bay. The Wild Pacific Trail offers an excellent opportunity for novice hikers to experience the natural beauty of the west coast. Numerous benches at scenic vistas present an opportunity to rest and simply watch the different moods of the sea. Signage is exceptional, with kilometer markers for every half a kilometer from the start.

The most often trod section is the first few kilometers around the Ucluth Peninsula, which features Amphitrite Point and Amphitrite Point Lighthouse. You can walk this as a loop trail, parking in one of the parking lots and then returning to your car by walking alongside Peninsula Road. To find the start of the trail, drive through Ucluelet and stay on Peninsula Road past the centre of town. Just past the junction of Peninsula and Coast Guard Road, you will see a parking lot that is reached by a short gravel road. A sign here depicts the location of the trail, and there are some nearby pit toilets. (Alternatively, turn right on Coast Guard Road and park in the lot near the point.)

Stairs at Big Beach, Wild Pacific Trail

The trail hugs the coast and allows for spectacular views towards Barkley Sound. If you are lucky, you might see whales feeding just offshore. This section around the peninsula is mostly gravel, with boardwalk in some places. You should reach Amphitrite Point Lighthouse, a very photogenic building, within about 20 minutes of easy walking. Amphitrite Point was named in 1859 after a ship, the HM *Amphitrite*. In Greek mythology, Amphitrite was one of the Nereids, or sea nymphs, a sea goddess and wife of Poseidon. The Amphitrite Point Lighthouse was first built here in 1906; the original lighthouse was lost in a tidal wave in 1914 and was immediately replaced. It has since been destaffed and decommissioned by the Canadian government. This point can receive some heavy seas during storms, and hikers are cautioned to remain on the trail. The point is also an area that is susceptible to rogue waves, which may catch you unaware.

Just east of Amphitrite Point is a small bay where the *Pass of Melfort* was lost with all hands on Christmas Day in 1905. This steel barque was bound from Panama to Port Townsend but missed the turnoff to the Strait of Juan de Fuca due to stormy seas and in a strong southwest gale ran aground here. More than fifty years after that ship met its watery end, a Greek freighter, the *Glafkos*, struck a reef of rocks close to Jenny Reef near Amphitrite Point on January 1, 1962, in a severe winter storm. The collision tore a 50-meter (160-foot) gash in the ship's hull and flooded the engine room. There ensued one of the most spectacular rescue missions ever to be witnessed on the west coast. With the assistance of two tugs from Victoria and vessels from the Life Saving Station in Bamfield, the *Glafkos* was salvaged with no loss of life. For a good read on this rescue, get a copy of Bruce Scott's book *Breakers Ahead!*, listed at the back of this book.

Once past the point, the path continues until you reach the boardwalks in He-Tin-Kis Park. There are some stairs in this area, so if any of your party is in a wheelchair, it is best to turn around at the lighthouse. At the end of this trail is a small parking lot and information on the park. To retrieve your vehicle, turn to the right along Peninsula Road and walk 5 minutes along the shoulder to kilometer 0.

The next phase of the trail from He-Tin-Kis plods along the sidewalk and shoulder of Peninsula Road until it intersects with Marine Drive. Turn left onto Marine Drive and walk along the gravel shoulder until it terminates. At time of publication this area was the scene of home construction and development. Should you want to avoid this portion of the trail, you could rejoin the Wild Pacific Trail at Big Beach, at kilometer marker 4.5, where there are a number of picnic tables along with pit toilets and parking for your vehicle. Follow the boardwalk and the trail signs to the west (your right as you face the ocean). There are some moderate elevation changes in this section. Just after the 6-kilometer marker, you will reach a temporary side trail that takes you to Cynamocka Road. Past this turnoff you will gain some elevation and be walking at the top of some steep cliffs. Watch your footing here and stay well back from the edge. The trail ends at kilometer 8.5, at the intersection with the bike path north of Ucluelet. There is a large map board of the trail at this trailhead, but at present very limited parking facilities. To return to your vehicle, retrace your steps or, if you parked in Ucluelet, back into town along the bike path. Keep to your left on this paved pathway and watch for bicyclists approaching from your rear.

Willowbrae Trail and Florencia Bay

> **SECTIONS AT A GLANCE**
> *Willowbrae Trail to Halfmoon Bay*
> DISTANCE: 2.8 km (1.7 miles) round trip · TIME: 1.5 hours
> RATING: 2 B II
> Beautiful secluded cove at the end

> *Willowbrae Trail to Florencia Beach*
> DISTANCE: 2.8 km (1.7 miles) round trip · TIME: 1.5 hours
> RATING: 2 B I
> Take some time to explore and walk along the beach

> *Florencia Beach from end of Willowbrae Trail*
> *to parking lot for Florencia Bay at northwest end*
> DISTANCE: 6.4 km (4 miles) one way · TIME: 2 hours · RATING: 1 A I
> Exercise caution in crossing Lost Shoe Creek. Some stairs at the north end of the beach to access the parking lot

Most of this trail lies within Pacific Rim National Park Reserve. To reach it from Ucluelet, turn left off the Pacific Rim Highway onto Willowbrae Road, a small signed gravel road about a 5-minute drive out of Ucluelet or about 5 kilometers (3 miles) south of the T junction with Highway 4. Follow the short gravel road to its end and a small parking area. The trail is on a well-groomed gravel path until you reach a Y junction. The left fork will take you down some 250 stairs and boardwalk ramps to Halfmoon Bay, a quiet cove. Here there is a small beach area with some beautiful tide pools among the rocks at the south end.

The right fork at the Y junction leads to Florencia Bay, a long strand of dark sand that stretches to the north towards Quisitis Point. The hike down to the beach is not difficult and consists of a series of wooden staircases. Florencia Bay is named after the *Florencia*, a

Long Beach, PHOTO BY A. DORST

Peruvian brigantine that was wrecked in this area on December 31, 1860. In his text on British Columbia coast names, Walbran reports that the ship's difficulties had commenced off Cape Flattery on November 12, when it was thrown on its beam ends in a gale wind. The vessel righted itself, but not before the captain, the cook and a passenger were drowned and the deck load, mainmast and foretopmast were lost. In this condition the *Florencia* sailed and drifted into Nootka Sound, where it was pumped out and found to be perfectly tight. The HM Gunboat *Forward* was sent to the ship's assistance and to tow the boat back to Victoria, but the *Forward* ran into trouble and the *Florencia* had to cast off, with the unfortunate result that after struggling with easterly gales, it was wrecked in Florencia Bay. The bay was called Wreck Bay due to this incident, and you may still hear locals call it by this name. The small island in the middle of the bay is Florencia Islet. It was used as a bombing target by the Royal

Canadian Air Force during World War II. For some years in the 1940s, a squatters' community of artists lived in handmade shelters and huts along Florencia Beach. They were evicted when the area became a national park in 1971.

When you enter the bay you are at the southeast end of the beach. By turning to your left you can explore the rocks near Wya Point, which separates Florencia Beach from Halfmoon Bay. In the winter California sea lions may be found here. If you turn to the right you can walk along the flat sand all the way towards Quisitis Point. During high tides, in winter months or at times of heavy water flows, you may encounter some difficulty in crossing Lost Shoe Creek. Parks Canada has closed access to the beach from Gold Mine Trail, which runs alongside this creek, since the bridge near its mouth kept being washed away during winter storms. The creek was named in 1903 by William Sutton, who lost a shoe there when he forded it. He cut a piece of cloth from his trousers and fashioned it into a makeshift moccasin. In such a way he was able to hike to Ucluelet. Near Lost Shoe Creek the sand is dark in color. A placer gold mine was in operation here upstream from the mouth of the creek in the early 1900s.

If you are successful at negotiating the creek without any loss of footwear, you can exit the beach area via a set of stairs that leads up to the parking lot for Florencia Bay. You can access this lot by turning off the Pacific Rim Highway onto the paved road that leads to the Wickaninnish Interpretive Centre.

Trails near Quisitis Point

> **TRAILS AT A GLANCE**
> *Nuu-chah-nulth Trail*
> DISTANCE: 2.5 km (1.5 miles) one way · TIME: 1.5 hours · RATING: 2 A
> Allow time to read informative signs. Most of the trail is on boardwalk

> *South Beach Trail*
> DISTANCE: 1.5 km (1 mile) round trip · TIME: 45 minutes
> RATING: 2 A I
> Most of the trail is on boardwalk

The major headland that separates Florencia Bay from Wickaninnish Bay is called Quisitis Point. There are two trails in this area, and both can be accessed from the Wickaninnish Interpretive Centre.

The Nuu-chah-nulth Trail connects Florencia Bay and Wickaninnish Bay; it was recently renovated with cedar boardwalks and is now a highlight of a visit to Pacific Rim National Park Reserve. It is an interpretive trail with stations and signage in English, French and Nuu-chah-nulth, the language of the local First Nation. For 2.5 kilometers (1.5 miles) the trail leads through the Quisitis headland area to the parking lot at Florencia Bay. One of the themes developed on the trail is *Hishuk ish ts'awalk,* or "Everything is one." You will be walking through some old-growth forest, and Canada's largest western hemlock is located near here. The trail was formerly known as the Wickaninnish Trail, after the great chief of the Tla-o-qui-aht who lived along this stretch of coast at the time of first European contact. There were three famous chiefs of the Pacific Northwest First Nations at time of contact. The other two were Maquinna, who lived to the north at Nootka Sound, and Tatoosh, from farther south on the Olympic Peninsula in Washington State.

If you are hiking from the Interpretive Centre, look for the start of the trail behind the building. For the first half kilometer (third of a mile) you will be on the same path as the South Beach Trail. The Nuu-chah-nulth Trail then turns to your left and continues for another 2 kilometers (1.2 miles). Remnants of an old wooden corduroy road can be seen at various spots as you walk through the mossy rain forest. Early settlers constructed these roads by placing and lining up small logs perpendicular to the direction of travel. They are termed corduroy since they resemble ridges on the fabric of the same name. The trail transects an interesting boggy area about midway along. The vast majority of the trail is on good boardwalk, the sole exception being some 200 meters (650 feet) near the east end, just before the parking lot at Florencia Bay.

The trail terminates at the Florencia Bay parking lot. You can either hike back in the same direction, walk back along the roads to the parking lot near the Wickaninnish Interpretive Centre or drive back if you are in a group with more than one car.

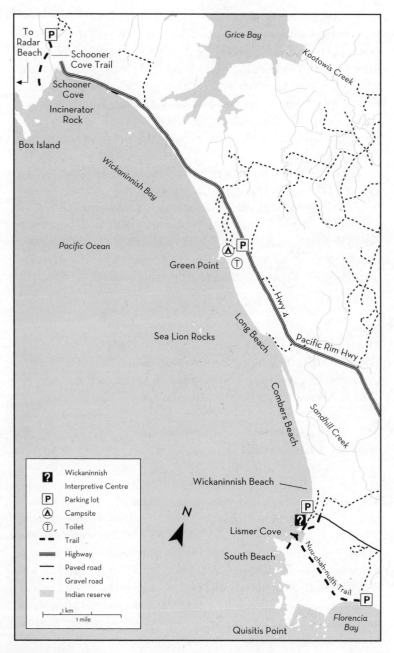

To
Radar
Beach

Schooner
Cove Trail

Schooner
Cove

Incinerator
Rock

Box Island

Wickaninnish Bay

Grice Bay

Kootowis Creek

Pacific Ocean

Green Point

Sea Lion Rocks

Long Beach

Hwy 4

Pacific Rim Hwy

Combers Beach

Sandhill Creek

Wickaninnish Beach

Lismer Cove

South Beach

Nuuchahnulth Trail

Florencia Bay

Quisitis Point

? Wickaninnish
Interpretive Centre
P Parking lot
Ⓐ Campsite
Ⓣ Toilet
- - - Trail
═══ Highway
─── Paved road
······ Gravel road
░░░ Indian reserve

1 km
1 mile

N

MAP 11: LONG BEACH TRAILS

The course of the South Beach Trail is the same as the Nuu-chah-nulth Trail for the first half kilometer. You will pass through groves of stunted Sitka spruce that have been shaped by the strong gales that whip in from the ocean. This trail parallels the shoreline and visits two secluded coves. The first one, called Lismer Cove, is named for Arthur Lismer, one of the Canadian Group of Seven painters who were famous for their impressionistic landscapes of the Canadian wilderness. He painted landscapes of the Pacific coast near here.

The cobbled beach can be slippery at times, so watch your footing carefully. The trail ascends from here and permits scenic views back to Wickaninnish Bay. After you pass the turnoff to the Nuu-chah-nulth Trail, you continue up along the boardwalk until you reach South Beach. Spend some time here and listen to the hissing sound that the stones make as the surf retreats. To your right there are some sea arches, which catch sea surges at the right height of the tide.

Long Beach Trails

> **TRAILS AT A GLANCE**

> *Wickaninnish Interpretive Centre to Schooner Cove*
DISTANCE: 18.4 km (11.4 miles) · TIME: 8–10 hours · RATING: 1 A 1
Tide problems on Combers Beach and at Green Point

> *Schooner Cove Trail*
DISTANCE: 1 km (0.6 mile) · TIME: 20–30 minutes · RATING: 2 A 1
Links Schooner Cove to parking lot

The sand seems to go on forever at Wickaninnish Bay. This 18-kilometer (11-mile) stretch of beach is famous worldwide for its incredible beauty. Although it is possible to hike all the way from the parking lot at the Wickaninnish Interpretive Centre north as far as Schooner Cove (and beyond at low tide), more often hikers park at one of the lots along the way and explore portions of the beach. The white sands of Long Beach have been attracting visitors to the coast for scores of years. When Highway 4 was completed in 1959, it opened up this area to the tourist trade. Particularly during the summer months, many visitors come to this part of the island. If you plan

Flores Island, PHOTO BY A. DORST

to stay at the Green Point campground, you should reserve your site well in advance. This campground operated by Parks Canada features drive-in campsites as well as primitive walk-in sites.

The Long Beach Unit of Pacific Rim National Park Reserve actually consists of three beach areas. From south to north they are Wickaninnish Beach, Combers Beach and Long Beach. If you plan on hiking the full length of these beaches, you should be aware that there will be some tide problems associated with getting across a small creek that empties onto Combers Beach. Walking around Green Point is also best done at low tide. However, there are bypass trails around Green Point through the camping area, so access is less of a problem than at Combers. As you get away from the parking lots and camping zones, you will experience quiet areas that are not as busy as the high-use areas. If you are walking all the way to Schooner Cove and are in a group with more than one vehicle, you can shuttle vehicles to return to your starting point.

Access to the Schooner Cove Trail is off Pacific Rim Highway, where there is a good-sized parking area. Follow the path through a cedar and hemlock forest along a well-maintained boardwalk. There are three elevation changes as you cross three small creeks. As you approach the beach you will enter a Sitka spruce forest. Descend to the wide sandy shoreline via a series of stairs. As you gain the beach you will see Box Island, a very photogenic spot. At low tide you can explore the rocks and tide pools at its base. Bird watching is quite good here. From Schooner Cove at low tides, it is possible to hike north and west to access Radar Beach. You may encounter slippery rocks and have some rock scrambling ahead of you to get around the point that separates Schooner Bay from Radar Beach. Schooner Cove is a particularly picturesque place. Camping was formerly permitted on the beach but the area received a significant amount of overuse and thus Parks Canada decided to limit access to day users only. The buildings to your left as you enter the beach are housing on Tla-o-qui-aht reserve land.

Trails Beyond Tofino

> **TRAILS AT A GLANCE**

> *Hot Springs Cove*
DISTANCE: 5 km (1.5 miles) round trip · TIME: 1–1.5 hours
RATING: 1 A
Some stairs to get to the hot springs. All on good boardwalk

> *Vargas Island telegraph trail*
DISTANCE: 6 km (3.7 miles) round trip · TIME: 3–4 hours
RATING: 2 B I
Access through private property at Vargas Island Inn

> *Wild Side Trail, Flores Island*
DISTANCE: 11 km (7 miles) one way · TIME: 3–6 hours · RATING: 2 B I
Time depends upon tide and trail conditions

> *Cow Bay to Mount Flores summit*
DISTANCE: 7 km (4.3 miles) round trip · TIME: 3–4 hours
RATING: 4 D I
Steep sections, rough route in part. Dicey log crossings

If you are into ecotourism, then Tofino is the right destination for you. There has been a proliferation of outfits that will take you to nearby locations to watch wildlife or to witness the stunning beauty of the west coast. Companies will guide you in a pampered style or simply drop you off on some deserted beach and return to pick you up again. Rather than listing a selection of these operators, I would urge you to do some comparison shopping on-line to find out what they offer and their rates. Three of the more common destinations that involve hiking are discussed here. Several trails are located on Vargas and Flores islands, to the north of Tofino.

> HOT SPRINGS COVE

Very few opportunities exist to experience thermal hot springs on the coast, so many visitors flock to Maquinna Marine Park each summer to soak in the warm waters of Hot Springs Cove. Numerous eco-tourism groups offer this opportunity as part of a wildlife-watching excursion out of Tofino. During the summer months you will need to book a spot in advance since these tours tend to fill up. Most tour operators provide you with passage in a good vessel with a knowledgeable tour guide who may also be the captain of your ship.

Your route out of Tofino may vary depending on weather conditions, but en route to the government dock at the cove, you will doubtless have been treated to sightings of sea mammals and marine birds. You will have a certain amount of time ashore once you reach the wharf, where there are pit toilets nearby. There are no designated camping facilities within the park, but the Hesquiaht Band operates a commercial campground to the north of the wharf. There is also a lodge and a floating bed and breakfast adjacent to the park. Note that recently BC Parks has started to charge a user fee (at this time $3 per person per day).

The trail to the hot springs, which takes you out along the Openit Peninsula, commences just past the information board. Generally it follows a First Nation trail that was then built upon by settlers. An upgrade to the trail was completed in 1995–97. The trail is entirely on boardwalk and is some 2.4 kilometers (1.5 miles) in length. There is the occasional short rise of stairs, plus a longer set of stairs at the hot springs. Many of the boards have been inscribed with the names of boats that have visited here over the years. Judging from the incredible detail and artwork on some of the boards, the owners and crew of some of these vessels must have spent some time in constructing their planks.

Most of the hiking is in the forest, with the occasional sea glimpse as you get closer to the hot springs. Allow about 30 minutes to hike in and slightly longer to hike back, since the elevation gain is against you on the return journey. The hot springs themselves begin in the forest and then descend in a cascading waterfall into small pools of decreasing temperature. The Nuu-chah-nulth called these springs Mak-she-kla-chuck, which can loosely be translated as "smoking waters."

There are changing facilities and toilets at the hot springs. Bathing suits at the springs themselves are required. Please note that the rocks in many places are very sharp and/or slippery, and sandals or runners should be worn when scrambling around. Use of soap and shampoo is banned in the pools. Although BC Parks suggests that bathers exercise caution when using the area during high tides, apparently one of the delights of soaking in the pools near the tide line is to receive a rush of ice cold water from the sea. A dip in the pools by the light of the full moon is also reported to be one of the most memorable events of many a summer vacation.

> **VARGAS ISLAND**

Vargas Island is about a 30-minute boat ride north by water taxi from the Tofino wharf. A 3-kilometer (1.8-mile) trail runs across the island from the dock at Vargas Island Inn, which offers the only accommodation and tent sites on the island. Phone 250-725-3309 for reservations. Ask permission from the innkeepers to cross their land. The trail follows an old telegraph line through bog and tussock. A corduroy road passes through this peat marshy area, but expect to encounter some wet areas, particularly if you step off the trail. Most of the trail lies within Vargas Island Provincial Park. Allow about an hour to reach the beautiful sandy beach at Ahous Bay. This was the site of an old aboriginal village of the same name. Before you set out to explore this beach, note or mark your entrance onto the beach, since the salal is quite thick here and you may have some difficulty finding the trail back to the east side of the island. There are no camping facilities on this beach. During the summer months you may see a resident gray whale that inhabits this bay. To the north and west of Ahous Bay, Cleland Island, an ecological reserve, is a bird sanctuary.

> **FLORES ISLAND**

The Wild Side Trail on Flores Island connects the First Nation village of Ahousat on the southeast side of the island to sandy beaches on the west side. This 11-kilometer (7-mile) trail was used by the

Ahousaht for many generations. Recently the trail has been upgraded and offers a wonderful opportunity for hikers to experience First Nations culture. Due to limited access to Flores Island, it may be difficult to do the whole trail as a day trip out of Tofino unless you have arranged transportation privately or with a tour operator.

The start of the trail is usually accessed via water taxi out of Tofino. The boat ride over to the wharf at Ahousat takes about 45 minutes. Ahousat in the Nuu-chah-nulth language means the "people with their backs to the land and the mountains" and reflects the location of the original village which was on the west side of Flores. It is now also the name of the present village site. The Nuu-chah-nulth themselves call their village Maaktusiis. There are some accommodations (a motel and hostel) north of the village. You should inform the boat's crew that you intend to hike the Wild Side Trail, and they will let you off at the hydro dock and phone ahead to let the caretaker of the trail know you are arriving.

From the dock, walk up the hill to the left to a dark brown building that houses the Maaktusiis General Store and a restaurant. The office for the Wild Side Trail is located on the left-hand side of the store in this building. The caretaker will have you sign a release of liability for hiking the trail and will ask for a donation to help maintain the trail. The suggested amount is $20 per person. An excellent guide written by Stanley Sam Sr., with information on the cultural significance of aspects of the trail, may be purchased in the office. Along the trail you will pass ten sites marked by hand-painted information boards that correspond to information contained in the guidebook. It is also possible to hire a First Nations guide who will accompany you and explain the cultural and natural history of the area.

To reach the start of the trail from the office, turn left along a gravel road and walk past a playing field and gymnasium. Turn right past the gym and then left again to go by the school and a small playing area. Walk along this gravel road until you reach a sign for the Wild Side Trail that points to your right near a log slash. Continue on this path until you see a sign indicating an industrial area. Turn left here and you will see the first signed site and a boardwalk that takes you across a boggy area. Once across this bog, follow a sandy path to cross a wide gravel logging road, then carry on down to the first beach area.

The trail follows a route that is full of history and meaning for the Nuu-chah-nulth. Hugging the coastline, it passes points of interest such as locations of spiritual importance, sites of First Nation conflicts and some culturally modified trees. You will visit and hike eight beaches along the way. The last beach area is at Cow Bay, where the trail turns inland to track Cow Creek and climbs to the summit of Mount Flores at 902 meters (2,960 feet). Cow Bay and Creek take their name from the cattle that were kept here by a settler named Edward Fitzpatrick in the early 1900s. Gray whales are often seen from this beach.

Most of the beach walking on this trail will be on good solid sand. The hike also includes forest routes on boardwalk over impassable headlands. The boardwalk at this time is in moderate shape but tends to get slippery when wet.

After about 1 1/2–2 hours of hiking, you should be between signed sites 5 and 6 where you may have to hike inland several kilometers to get across a stream over a silver bridge. If the tide is right, and you have consulted tide tables, you can take the shortcut over the headland, which represents the southeast tip of the point that separates Whitesand Cove from the bay to the west. The trip through the forest will add about 90 minutes to your trip.

The route to the summit of Mount Flores will take you about 2 hours. The trail is not as well maintained as the path that follows the beaches, so be prepared for log crossings, steep terrain and rougher conditions. This part of the trail is not recommended for novices.

The rehabilitation of the aboriginal path began in 1993 when a group of Ahousaht formed an organization called Walk the Wild Side with the intent of promoting the trail as an ecotourism destination. As word of the incredible beaches, lush green forests and wildlife spread through the hiking community of the west coast, thousands made the trip and the effects of their passage were felt on the land. The trail had begun to deteriorate by the mid-1990s, and there was a growing concern among the Ahousaht elders over environmental damage and spoiling of their ancestral sites. In 1996 a joint venture between the Ahousaht Band Council and the Western Canada Wilderness Committee hired First Nations youth to perform trail upgrades and install cedar boardwalks.

6

THE NOOTKA
TRAIL

· · · · ·

> **TOTAL DISTANCE:** 35 km (22 miles)

> **TOTAL TIME:** 3–5 days

> **AVERAGE RATING:** 3 B III

> **ACCESS:** Highway 28 (from Campbell River) to Gold River, then Air Nootka floatplane service to Louie Lagoon or Yuquot (Friendly Cove). MV *Uchuck III* serves Yuquot from Gold River, as do water taxis.

> **HAZARDS:** Tides, steep inclines from beach, slippery boulders

> **SPECIAL FEATURES:** Waterfall, fossils, beach walks, ocean views, sea stacks, First Nations heritage sites, sea otters, whales, historic sites, sea caves

> **MAPS 1:20,000:** 092E076 (Ferrer Point) · 092E066 (Bajo Point) · 092E067 (Boston Point) · 092E057 (Maquinna Point) **1:50,000:** 92E10 (Nootka)

> **TIDE TABLES:** Zone 12. Use tables for Saavedra Islands.

> *Louie Lagoon trailhead to Third Beach*
> DISTANCE: 1 km (0.6 mile) · TIME: 30–40 minutes · RATING: 1 B I
> Meanders through easy terrain

> *Third Beach to Calvin Falls*
> DISTANCE: 11 km (7 miles) · TIME: 4–5 hours · RATING: 3 C III
> Some steep sections over impassable headlands

> *Calvin Falls to Beano Creek*
> DISTANCE: 11 km (7 miles) · TIME: 3–4 hours · RATING: 1 A III
> Can be done mostly on the beach

> *Beano Creek to Maquinna Point*
> DISTANCE: 7 km (4.3 miles) · TIME: 4–5 hours · RATING: 3 C III
> Potential water shortage in dry summers

> *Maquinna Point to Yuquot*
> DISTANCE: 5 km (3 miles) · TIME: 2–3 hours · RATING: 3 B III
> Scenic vistas

> ACCESS AND PERMITS

Getting to this hike along the west coast of Nootka Island can be a bit pricey. The usual starting place is Gold River, which is reached via Highway 28 from Campbell River. Most hikers fly from Gold River to the northern end at Louie Lagoon and then hike south to Yuquot (Friendly Cove), where they catch the MV *Uchuck III* back to Gold River. There are accommodations and pubs in the town of Gold River. Camping is found along the road that leads to the government wharf west of the townsite. For information on lodging and camping, visit the information centre to your right as you enter the town. Parking is found along the side of the road to the government wharf.

Air access is commercially supplied by Air Nootka from its floating dock at the mouth of the Gold River. Rates will vary depending upon the type of aircraft you will need for your party. You should phone for reservations, 250-283-2255, or visit their Web site at www.airnootka.com for their rates. Their Web site also contains information on and a gallery of aerial shots of the Nootka Trail.

If you plan to catch the *Uchuck III* either to or from Yuquot (Friendly Cove) in the summer, you should make reservations, since space on the vessel is limited. Obviously you should also consult its schedule for pickup from Friendly Cove. At this time during the summer months, the *Uchuck* visits Yuquot (Friendly Cove) on Wednesdays and Saturdays. Further information is available from Nootka Sound Service Ltd., the operators of the *Uchuck III*, at 250-283-2325 or 250-283-2515. Their Web site, www.mvuchuck.com, contains information on schedules and rates. As an alternative, it is possible to hire water taxis from the harbor at Gold River. Inquire at the information centre in town for names of operators and rates.

Hikers should be aware that the Mowachaht-Muchalaht First Nation will charge a fee of $40 per person for crossing their land at Yuquot. This fee allows for passage over their land as well as visiting the church and camping on site. It also allows for hiking their system of trails known as Yatz-mahs. For up-to-date information on fees, please contact the Mowachaht Band in Gold River at 250-283-2015 or toll-free at 1-800-238-2933.

If you are stuck in Yuquot or need emergency assistance, there are radio phones at Ray Williams's house on the reserve, at the custodian's office at the back of the church and at the lighthouse. There is no coverage for cell phones on the Nootka Trail.

> **TRAIL DESCRIPTION AND HISTORY**

The west side of Nootka Island is steeped in history. For centuries the Nuu-chah-nulth people lived off the riches and resources of this coast. When the Europeans, Spanish and very soon after that the British arrived on the west coast of Vancouver Island, Nootka Island and Nootka Sound were the areas of first contact with the Nuu-chah-nulth. For a brief time in the late eighteenth century, the lucrative fur trade between the two cultures sparked interest in the area on the world stage. When the focus shifted away from trade and onto colonization, the island returned to less tumultuous times and the European settlers headed for the far less wild shores of the east coast of Vancouver Island. But Nootka Island remains, still wild and relatively unspoiled—and a treat and prime destination for the hiker.

This is the only trail in this guide whose protection status is in some doubt at the time of publication. The hike is mostly on Crown land which has an uncertain future, but the trail also passes through privately held and Indian reserve lands. The area has been used for thousands of years by the Mowachaht. Stories tell of the women from the band traveling from Yuquot to do their laundry at Calvin Falls.

As long ago as the mid-seventies hikers from Strathcona Park Lodge School began to explore and lay out the trail. In the 1980s groups of hikers were flown into Crawfish Lake and made their way from the lake to visit the beach area near Calvin Falls. Gradually more groups explored and linked the beaches together with trails around headlands. Within the last decade, the area was promoted by the Federation of Mountain Clubs of British Columbia to enable hikers to experience the beauty of the area and to help conservation efforts at achieving protection status for the area. With the publicity of the hike through its appearance in a hiking magazine in the mid-nineties, the area became much more popular. Today the Nootka Trail is visited by a large number of hikers each summer. An estimated 1,000 hiked the trail in 2004.

Most hikers walk the route in one direction only, from north to south, which is how it is described in this chapter. It is also possible to hike in from Friendly Cove to Third Beach and then back again. Although the trail can be hiked in 3–5 days, allow longer for rest days and exploring.

If you fly in to Louie Lagoon (also known as Starfish Lagoon), your pilot will drop you off in ankle- to shin-deep water at the south end of the lagoon. You should wear shorts and sandals and expect to ferry your packs to land from the floatplane. If the weather is clear on your flight in, you will be able to spot much of the trail in an abbreviated fashion from the air. The start of the trail and indeed the whole trail to Third Beach is well marked in the forest with tape and orange flashers nailed to trees. Follow this trail for approximately 30–45 minutes until you emerge alongside the creek that flows out to the sea at Third Beach.

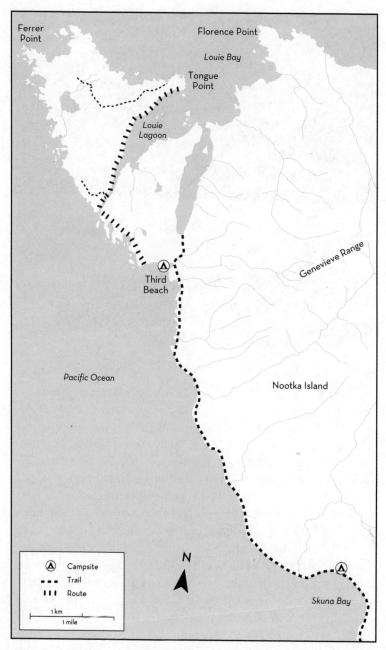

MAP 12: NOOTKA TRAIL—LOUIE LAGOON TO SKUNA BAY

Third Beach

Third Beach is a delightful place to camp. Most campsites are located in the driftwood above the high-water mark. There are some fixed ropes in place for bear caches. Water is available from the creek at the south end of the beach. Many hikers stop here after their first easy hike in, so the place tends to get crowded. You can make exploratory day trips from Third Beach to see areas around the mud flats located to the west of Louie Bay and the wreck of a Greek freighter at Tongue Point. It is also possible to bushwhack towards a radar installation, a relic left over from World War II, near Ferrer Point. To reach these areas, follow Third Beach to its northern end and look for the start of the trail marked by buoys among the salal and brush. Be aware that you may encounter a tide problem at a narrow channel along the trail to the mud flats. You should hike here on a lowering tide and plan to get back to this location before the tide reaches a level of 1.7 meters (5.6 feet).

From Third Beach you may elect to hike around the point just beyond the creek at the south end of the beach and most of the way along the coast to Calvin Falls if the tide is low enough. However, some headlands en route are better crossed by using bypass trails in the forest. If the tide is high you will have to hike in the forest for much of the way. The forest hiking is marked exceptionally well with bright orange metal flashers and tape. The forest trail is, generally speaking, a well-used trail and should pose little difficulty unless it is muddy. The hiking along the coast can vary depending upon the type of beach encountered.

If you do not have low enough tides to hike the beach route, you must gain access to the forest trail by hiking up the steep incline inland which is at the south end of Third Beach. There is a fixed rope here to help you climb the slope. As is the case with all such ropes and aids, make sure you test it to ensure it is solid. It takes 4 or 5 hours depending upon your route to reach Calvin Falls. There is camping north of the falls in Skuna Bay, but water can be a problem during dry summers. Be prepared to filter or boil all water sources along the trail. If the tide is low enough, you will be able to hike around the headland that separates Skuna Bay from the beach at Calvin Falls.

You will be nearly upon the falls before you spot them nestled among some trees. The falls are picturesque and this is a good spot to bathe, so it tends to get very crowded during hot weather. Remember your camping etiquette here and allow some space between groups. There is a shelter in the woods to the north of the falls off a short trail that is well marked with buoys. Unless it is pelting down with rain, the beach camping is preferable. Remains of fossilized leaves may be seen in the rock slabs south of the falls. It is possible with the assistance of a rope to walk up to the top of the falls via the right-hand side as you face them. However, it is neither easily possible nor recommended to hike alongside Calvin Creek to Crawfish Lake. If you are interested in gaining access to the lake, a very rough trail starts at the south end of the beach past the falls.

The stretch of trail between Calvin Falls and Beano Creek can all be done on the beach, although the conditions vary. From Calvin Falls you will experience at first easy beach walking on packed sand. Once you reach the point at the end of the sandy beach, your easy hiking is over. You will start to encounter boulders and rocks of various shapes and sizes. These rocky areas tend to be slippery, and it is imperative that you watch your footing here. A hiking pole or two may assist you in balancing on small boulders, but it is best to go slowly through these sections rather than risk a twisted ankle or worse.

After a few hours of walking you will reach Bajo Point. Bajo Point is delineated by a large sea stack located offshore. It was named by Captain Malaspina; the Spanish word *bajo* means "below" and refers to the reef that extends southward from the point. Over the years the area has seen its share of shipwrecks and is considered a navigational hazard. At low tides it is possible to hike out to the point to explore some of the sea life or to search for sea otters. These marine mammals were nearly extirpated due to the trade in their pelts. In 1911 a number of countries, including Great Britain on behalf of Canada, signed a treaty to ban their hunting. Since then the sea otter has been making a slow comeback. From 1969 to 1972, the species was reintroduced to the west coast of Vancouver Island. Today their population is estimated to be 2,000 animals on the island's west coast, ranging from east of Cape Scott to Estevan Point to the south. You may spot this elusive creature resting or feeding on its back in sea kelp from Bajo Point south towards Maquinna Point.

Inland from Bajo Point, a small, barely distinct trail takes you across the tall beach grass and into the forest, which was once the site of a Mowachaht village. At one time, there were longhouses here and a thriving community. Now little remains but ferns overgrowing the mounds where structures once stood. Please respect this land and do not disturb anything. This area is an Indian reserve called Aass.

The walking past Bajo is on pebble beaches of varying dimensions of stone and rock. This can make for tedious going. Also the pebbles have a tendency to climb up over the tops of boots and nestle among the inner recesses of your feet. If you haven't done so already, this would be a good time to rummage in your pack and pull out the gaiters you were reserving for muddy sections of the trail.

At present a large sand spit protects the mouth of Beano Creek and allows for relatively easy crossings at low tide. However, this configuration is apt to change during a severe winter storm, when the entire area can be reconfigured.

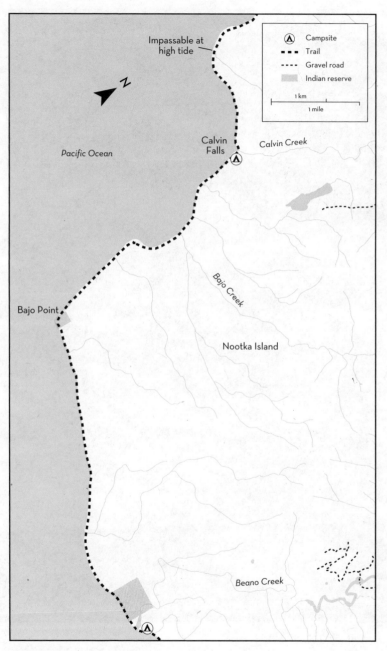

Impassable at
high tide

Calvin
Falls

Calvin Creek

Pacific Ocean

Campsite
Trail
Gravel road
Indian reserve

1 km
1 mile

Bajo Creek

Bajo Point

Nootka Island

Beano Creek

MAP 13: NOOTKA TRAIL—SKUNA BAY TO BEANO CREEK

Nootka Island, PHOTO BY A. DORST

Beano Creek was named after Albert Bean, who owned a cabin in a cleared area near the mouth of the creek in 1914. The creek is a great place to swim. If you need water, walk some distance upstream where the water is less brackish.

There are some private dwellings on the south side of Beano Creek. These homes are posted as private property and ought not to be used by passing hikers.

The trail from Beano Creek leads south along the beach until you reach an area of coast bordered by gray cliffs. Two trails lead up from this area to flank impassable headlands to your south. If the tide is right, you can reach the farther trail. It goes into a smallish cove past a dank, slippery rock area and up some equally slippery moss slopes that you ascend with the aid of a rope to reach the forest trail. If the tide is too high for you to access this point, you should take the first access trail that you reach. Here you will have to do some moderate to strenuous bushwhacking to rejoin the trail at the juncture of the second access trail. The start of this first trail is located in a bowl-like depression in the cliffs and is marked by some floats and sea urchin husks suspended on a bit of rope.

Potable water may be a potential problem during a dry summer on the trail towards Maquinna Point. The best place to fill your water containers is Callicum Creek, which you will reach about 1 hour out of Beano Creek. Callicum was the name of a fellow chief and close friend of the great Chief Maquinna. He was shot by the Spanish when he protested their occupation of Nootka Sound in 1789.

Just past the creek you will descend to a small beach. At tides above 1.6 meters (5 feet) you may experience some difficulty in getting around a rocky cliff area. The trail from here links up some pocket beaches. After about 45 minutes of hiking you will arrive at the top of a cliff with views out to the south. From here, you should also be able to spot two beaches. The smaller first beach has a large dark rock that bears a resemblance to the profile of a man's head. There may be a small waterfall at the north end of this beach. There is good camping here above the high-water mark.

If there is no water source on this beach, then you should push on to the second beach. You can access this beach by scuttling around the rocky headland at low tide or by taking the bypass trail over the headland at high tide. About two-thirds of the way down this beach there is a campsite within the forest with a small trail leading from the site to a water source. If you do press on towards Maquinna Point, your options for camping are limited due to lack of water supply during dry summers. Some hikers choose to replenish all water containers at Callicum Creek and lug the water to a choice camping area on a beach above the high-water mark.

Most groups stop somewhere on the way to Maquinna Point. Depending upon where you have camped for the night, it may be another 1 to 2 hours' hike before you reach the point itself. You will mostly be hiking in the forest or along the tops of cliffs with fantastic sea views. Just before you reach the junction to Maquinna Point, you will see a trail signed "Lake" that leads eastward down to a small lake. Access to the lake for swimming purposes is difficult due to dead trees that line the shore. However, it is possible to obtain water here.

The next junction you will reach is the side trail that leads to Maquinna Point. It is recommended that you drop your packs at the intersection and hike 10 minutes to the point. You can scramble among the rocks for great views south to the Hesquiaht Peninsula and north to Beano. During the fishing season, numerous sport fishing vessels try their luck just offshore. A large wooden triangle demarks fishing zones. The point is named for the great chief of the Mowachaht people.

Back on the trail from the point you will again be in the forest for much of the way to a tidal lagoon. En route to this location and about 45 minutes past the Maquinna Point turnoff, you will encounter another side trail, marked "Caves." Descend 5 minutes along this trail to a beach to find three sea-carved caves that would make excellent camping in a rainstorm. There is no water source here, however, so camping may be a bit of a logistical problem. In about 10 minutes' hike from the cave trail junction, you will descend to a small pocket beach and get your first glimpse of Yuquot. About an hour past the caves you will come to one of the last obstacles you will face before reaching Friendly Cove. This is a stream called Tsa'tsil by the Mowachaht. Its name means "where the tide comes up and goes into the lagoon." The creek does indeed come out of a tidal lagoon and can only be safely forded during low tides. The

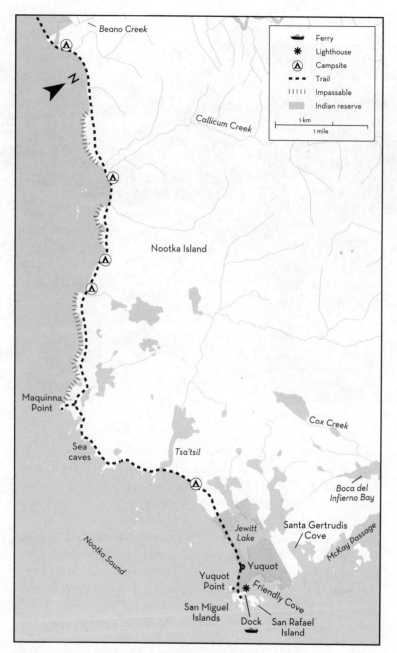

MAP 14: NOOTKA TRAIL—BEANO CREEK TO FRIENDLY COVE

Legend:
- Ferry
- Lighthouse
- Campsite
- Trail
- Impassable
- Indian reserve

1 km
1 mile

Beano Creek
Callicum Creek
Nootka Island
Maquinna Point
Sea caves
Tsa'tsil
Cox Creek
Boca del Infierno Bay
Nootka Sound
Jewitt Lake
Santa Gertrudis Cove
McKay Passage
Yuquot
Yuquot Point
Friendly Cove
San Miguel Islands
Dock
San Rafael Island

Beano Creek, PHOTO BY A. DORST

crossing is best done about 50 meters (160 feet) in from the mouth. Wear sandals, since the mussels and barnacles in this area can be quite sharp and cause cuts. Depending upon the level of the tide, your crossing should be anywhere from ankle to waist deep. The water here is brackish and not fit for consumption.

The land above the high-water mark is privately owned. At high tides this stream is a great place to swim and clean off the grime from your hike. Walk along the beach past Tsa'tsil until you reach a large triangular-shaped sea stack. There is a small creek and camping spot here, which is just off the Indian reserve land. This area was called Mowinis by the Mowachaht. Just past Mowinis, you can leave the beach for faster hiking along the Yatz-mahs ("walk around") trails to

Yuquot. You may choose instead to walk along the pebble beach all the way to the church, but by this time you may wish for terrain with firmer footing.

If you do take the trail, you will see some cabins alongside Aa-aak-quaksius Lake, also known as Jewitt Lake, that are for rent during the summer months. Jewitt Lake is named for John Jewitt, a nineteen-year-old English blacksmith/armorer from a Boston trading ship who was taken into slavery by Maquinna in 1803. His account of his years spent with the Mowachaht makes for fascinating reading. If you are interested in staying in one of the cabins, inquire at the band office at the back of the church. As you walk the trail towards Yuquot you will pass a cemetery on your left. Access to this cemetery is not permitted.

Yuquot means "the place where the wind blows in all directions." It was the summer home of the Mowachaht, who came here from Tahsis, their winter residence. Yuquot was "discovered" by Captain Cook, who visited here in 1778 with his two ships the *Discovery* and the *Resolution*. This visit represented the first land-based contact between Europeans and the First Nations of the west coast of British Columbia. The Spanish had explored the coast in this area four years prior to Cook's visit but had not set foot on shore. A few years after Cook landed at Yuquot, the Spanish occupied the area and built a settlement that they named Santa Cruz de Nutka. They also built a fort on a nearby island.

A period of conflict between the Spanish and English over Nootka Sound was eventually resolved through the signing of the Nootka Convention of 1790, in which the Spanish gave up any claim to the area. In 1792 Captain George Vancouver and commander Juan Francisco de la Bodega y Quadra met here, picnicked and discussed how best to implement the terms of the convention.

For a time Yuquot was the most important port on the west coast north of Mexico due to the trade in sea otter pelts, which caused the population of sea otters to decline to nearly disastrous levels in only forty years from 1780. When the trade in pelts ceased, the British established their base of operations for Vancouver Island in Victoria.

Most of the residents of the Yuquot area were relocated by the Canadian government to the mouth of the Gold River in 1968, but during the summer some members of the Mowachaht-Muchalaht

First Nation still use Yuquot as a seasonal camp. Several sites in the area are well worth visiting, including a church that has been in the same location since 1875, although the original was replaced in 1956 by the present one. On display in the church are totem poles, replicas of house posts, wood carvings and a visual presentation of the history of the area. Two stained-glass windows, a gift from the Spanish people, grace both sides of the entranceway.

The only year-round occupant of the area, Ray Williams, may be found at his home on the leeward side of the peninsula. His son Sanford Williams is a master carver who creates wooden masks and other works of art for sale. If you are flying back to Gold River, you should contact Ray to make a radiophone call to Air Nootka, and you will catch your return flight from the floating dock in front of his home. He charges a small docking fee.

Should you have some time before you catch your transport back to Gold River, ask one of the First Nations custodians to point out the location of an old totem pole that is no longer standing. This is the totem pole that Chief Napoleon Maquinna presented to the governor general of Canada, Lord Willingdon, on his visit along with British Columbia Lieutenant Governor Randolph Bruce to Yuquot in 1929. Lord Willingdon could not take the totem pole with him so he presented it back to the village. When the governor general received the totem pole, there was some expectation that a gift would be given or a potlatch hosted in return. Through an interpreter, Lieutenant Governor Bruce learned that the chief and community greatly desired a chain saw, so one was sent later on by the steamer *Maquinna*, which serviced these small communities for many years. Now the totem pole lies amid salal and blackberry bush. The Mowachaht believe it should lie in rest undisturbed where it fell.

The lighthouse is one of the few remaining lighthouses in Canada that is staffed. It was built in 1911 and is reached by boardwalk on the east side of Yuquot. If you have a reservation to catch the MV *Uchuck III* back to Gold River, plan to be at the government wharf near the lighthouse early enough to ensure that you can get on board.

7

CAPE SCOTT PROVINCIAL PARK AND AREA

· · · · ·

> **TOTAL DISTANCE:** 29 km (18 miles) (Cape Scott only, one way)

> **TOTAL TIME:** 3–4 days; allow extra time to explore

> **AVERAGE RATING:** 2 C I

> **ACCESS:** Highway 19 north (from Campbell River), then 64 km (40 miles) of rough gravel logging roads west from near Port Hardy to Holberg and beyond

> **HAZARDS:** Tides, slippery boardwalks, muddy conditions

> **SPECIAL FEATURES:** Sea stacks, sea caves, beach walks, remains of early settlement, lighthouse, wildlife viewing

> **MAPS 1:20,000:** 1021069 (Helen Islands) · 1021078 (Cape Scott) · 1021079 (Rasmus Creek) · 1021089 (Christensen Point) **1:50,000:** 102109 (San Josef) · 102116 (Cape Scott)

> **TIDE TABLES:** Zone 15. Use tide tables for Cape Scott.

Cape Scott Provincial Park

> **SECTIONS AT A GLANCE**

> *Trailhead to San Josef Bay*
DISTANCE: 2.5 km (1.5 miles) · TIME: 45 minutes · RATING: 1 B I
Wheelchair accessible and suitable for families

> *Trailhead to Eric Lake*
DISTANCE: 3 km (2 miles) · TIME: 1 hour · RATING: 2 D
Recent trail improvements but can still be muddy

> *Eric Lake to Fisherman River*
DISTANCE: 6.3 km (4 miles) · TIME: 2 hours · RATING: 2 D
Passes through old-growth forest—expect muddy conditions

> *Fisherman River to Hansen Lagoon*
DISTANCE: 5.4 km (3.4 miles) 2 hours · RATING: 2 C
Allow time to explore the remains of settlement

> *Fisherman River to Nissen Bight*
DISTANCE: 5.7 km (3.5 miles) · TIME: 2.5 hours · RATING: 2 C II
Expect mud from the trail junction to the beach

> *Fisherman River to Nels Bight*
DISTANCE: 7.5 km (4.7 miles) · TIME: 3 hours · RATING: 1 B II
Most hikers use this beach as a base camp for further exploration

> *Nels Bight to Experiment Bight*
DISTANCE: 2.1 km (1.3 miles) · TIME: 30 minutes · RATING: 1 B II
Very scenic

> *Experiment Bight to Guise Bay*
DISTANCE: 1 km (0.6 mile) · TIME: 20 minutes · RATING: 1 B II
Follows old plank road to a beautiful beach

> *Guise Bay to Cape Scott Lighthouse*
DISTANCE: 3 km (2 miles) · TIME: 1 hour · RATING: 2 B
Not possible to hike to the cape; the lighthouse is the usual
stopping destination

NOTE: These distances and times are one way only, and the times are for good weather conditions.

> ## ACCESS AND PERMITS

Follow Highway 19 north from Campbell River about 208 kilometers (125 miles). About 2 kilometers (1.2 miles) before you reach Port Hardy, Holberg Road branches off Highway 19 on your left. Check your gas gauge, since the gas station in Holberg is not always open. If in doubt, gas up in Port Hardy. After a few hundred meters the road turns into gravel. It can be rough for the next 60 kilometers (37 miles), with many potholes and washboard sections. There are a number of active logging areas off Holberg Road, so be prepared to meet loaded logging trucks during regular working hours.

After you pass Holberg, the road to Cape Scott is known as San Josef Mainline and it gets steadily narrower. Follow the signs for Cape Scott Provincial Park and you should eventually arrive at a parking lot at the end of the road. Space is limited at the present time, although BC Parks advises that there are plans to expand the parking lot. There have been reports of vandalism and thefts in the parking lot, and some hikers prefer to leave their vehicle at San Josef Heritage Park, a commercial campground to your left just before you arrive at the trailhead. This is run by Doug DesJarlais (phone number 250-288-3682). For a nominal fee he will let you park and will also take you to the trailhead.

If you arrive too late to hike to the Eric Lake or San Josef Bay camping areas, limited car camping is available at a Western Forest Products site that you would have passed en route to the trailhead parking lot; car camping is also available at San Josef Heritage Park.

To reach Raft Cove Provincial Park or Cape Palmerston recreation area, take the Ronning Mainline logging road to your left at the intersection with San Josef Mainline and follow the signs to either location. There is very limited parking available at the trailhead to Raft Cove. Make sure your vehicle does not block someone else from exiting. Cape Palmerston has an ample-sized parking area.

BC Parks charges a backcountry camping fee of $5 per person per day for overnight stays in the park. You may pay at the self-registration vaults at the trailhead at the end of the parking lot. There are no fees for camping at Raft Cove or Cape Palmerston recreation area.

The northwest part of Vancouver Island is a magical spot. It is incredibly wild and can receive some of the most severe weather the coast of Vancouver Island ever experiences. It is also one of the wettest areas on the island. Notwithstanding the harsh conditions, settlers attempted to form a community here at the turn of the twentieth century. Their story will unfold before you as you trek the same trails as these hardy people did more than 100 years before you. Expect to encounter mud on the trail unless the weather has been dry for some time. BC Parks has recently improved portions of the trail through the construction of boardwalks over the roughest areas. However, the trail still contains sections that are not easy and are apt to be more difficult in wet weather.

First Nations people used this area from time immemorial. The Quatsino and Tlatlasikwala have claimed the land around Cape Scott itself. Some of the groups of First Nations who inhabited this area were particularly hard hit by disease after contact with Europeans. The Yutlinuk of the Scott Islands died out in the nineteenth century.

Cape Scott was first explored by Europeans in 1786 when two British vessels, the *Captain Cook* and the *Experiment,* captained by Henry Lowrie and John Guise, respectively, traveled here on a trading and exploration expedition. The cape was named after David Scott, a merchant from either Canton or Bombay who financially backed the voyage. Both captains' names and the name of one of the vessels were subsequently given to two bays and a bight along the nearby coast.

When British Columbia joined Canada in 1871, it embarked upon a program to encourage immigration into the newly formed province. It opened up vast tracts of Crown land for pre-emption by settlers. This era saw a number of movements to the west coast by Scandinavian groups. A group of Norwegians settled in the Quatsino and Bella Coola areas, and a group of Finns emigrated to Sointula, on Malcolm Island. Beginning in 1896 the Cape Scott area was the site of an attempt by Danes to form a long-term settlement.

Rasmus Hansen was one of the leaders of this first group of Danes. His name now lives on in the lagoon that he initially explored on a

Macjack River, Raft Cove

fishing trip out of Seattle. The story of this group's attempt to carve homes and livelihoods out of the wilderness at the far tip of Vancouver Island is a fascinating read, and the interested hiker should attempt to find a copy of *The Cape Scott Story*, by Lester Peterson, which unfortunately is no longer in print. The original point of disembarkation for these intrepid settlers was Fisherman Bay, at the north end of the park. The settlers had extracted a promise from the provincial government that a road would be constructed between Fisherman Bay and Sea Otter Cove. That road was never built. However, the remains of the original road that was built from Fisherman Bay to the diked-in areas to the east of Hansen Lagoon can still be walked today if you descend to Nissen Bight. The colonizers spent much labor in constructing the dike to keep out the tides at Hansen

Forest mist

Lagoon. This land, which is now grassy, was routinely flooded at high tides before the dikes were built.

The Danes built a store and schoolhouse as well as other structures. Eventually the lack of suitable transportation, poor harbors, and the province's failure to provide, as promised, more land for pre-emption, plus the harsh conditions, were sufficient to persuade many of the original settlers to leave. By 1907 many had departed for pre-emptions farther south, along Quatsino Sound or at Holberg.

Around the same time as these first immigrants were leaving for more placid waters, other prospective settlers from Europe and the United States were reading lyrical accounts of the settlement in newspapers in the American Midwest. One such reader was Henry Ohlsen, who had just been told by his doctor that due to his advanced tuberculosis he had only six months to live. His doctor cautioned him to move to a dry climate. He chose to leave Iowa with his family and move to San Josef Bay! He lasted considerably longer than the six months allotted to him: a store he ran at the mouth of the San Josef River was in business until 1944. The provincial government of the day opened up more land for pre-emption, and others moved into the area that had been vacated by the first group. This time their community was established farther west of Fisherman Bay.

The same problems with remoteness and lack of road access that had plagued the Danes led to the gradual disintegration of this community as well. Many left when the men were conscripted during World War I. However, pockets of homesteads near San Josef Bay and Hansen Lagoon persisted until after the 1940s. During World War II, a radar installation and several buildings were constructed on the isthmus near the cape known as the sand neck. These facilities were evacuated after the war, and the last homestead, the Spencer farm near Hansen Lagoon, was vacated in 1956.

In 1973, Cape Scott Provincial Park was created. Over the years, the size of the park has increased, most notably with the 1995 addition of the Nahwitti-Shushartie Corridor. Now the park is the third largest on Vancouver Island.

Many of the trails you will hike in Cape Scott Provincial Park are remnants of the old settlement roads and trails. The trails begin at the small parking lot, which may be full during the summer months.

Two large notice boards at the trailhead are worth your study, since tide tables and information about recent bear and cougar sightings will be posted here. Notices on trail conditions are also posted from time to time.

If you are hiking to San Josef Bay, turn left at a T intersection about 1 kilometer (0.6 mile) from the trailhead. The trail to San Josef is easy and is either graveled or boardwalk until you reach the beach. When you reach the San Josef River, turn to the right to hike out to the beach. At this right-hand turn BC Parks has installed an information board by a side trail that leads through the thick bush to the site of Henry Ohlsen's store and trading post. Continue past this turnoff and cross a wooden bridge. A few minutes past this bridge you will find camping sites, toilets and food caches on the first beach you come to. At low tide you can walk along this beach to the rocky point and walk between sea stacks and past sea caves to the second beach, where there are also camping sites and pit toilets. The second beach is not accessible at high tide from the first beach. The rough access trail over the headland has been closed by BC Parks.

From the second beach it is possible to take a very rugged, unmaintained trail up to Mount St. Patrick. If the day is clear, the views from the top of this summit crowned by dwarf juniper and crowberry are spectacular. The trees on this apex are all stunted and contorted from the high winds and rough weather. It is possible to hike down the north side of Mount St. Patrick to Sea Otter Cove, then continue by a rough route to a beautiful beach at Lowrie Bay. If you do this, you should know that the route down the north side of Mount St. Patrick is not well defined and is rather steep in sections.

Sea Otter Cove is named after a vessel, the *Sea Otter*, that was captained by James Hanna. No suitable camping is available in this dank and dark cove, which is very muddy. A rough trail leads out of the cove, but note that the creek here floods on a high tide, making the route-finding a bit tricky. The route leads to a fine white shell and sand beach at Lowrie Bay. None of these routes are well maintained by BC Parks. If you choose to hike here you should expect very rugged conditions, including steep grades, fallen trees and mud, in all but the driest of seasons. This hike is not recommended for novices; only a few adventurous souls are likely to try it on an annual

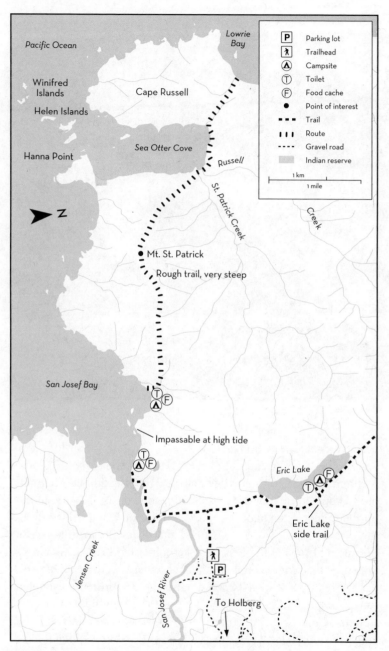

MAP 15: CAPE SCOTT TRAIL—SAN JOSEF RIVER TO ERIC LAKE

Near Guise Bay, PHOTO BY A. DORST

basis. Budget 4 hours to reach Sea Otter Cove from San Josef Bay and another 1.5 hours to get to Lowrie Bay from the cove.

From the trailhead, turn right at the T intersection on the main trail if your destination is Cape Scott or one of the beaches at the northern end of the park. The first camping area you will reach in this direction is at Eric Lake, named after Eric Christensen, one of the adopted sons of the first local schoolmaster, Carl Brink Christensen. At that time a certain number of students were required in order to open up a school. To achieve the quota, Christensen adopted sons Eric and William. Eric died when the community's transport ship, the *Cape Scott*, went down en route to Quatsino in 1910. The family lives on in local place names such as Eric Lake, William Lake and Brink Lake. At one time Eric Lake was misnamed Erie Lake by cartographers for the provincial government in Victoria, and you may still see this name on older maps of the Cape Scott area.

Eric Lake is a good place to stay if you got started on the trail late in the day. Here you will find platforms for tents, a source for drinking water (all water in the park should be treated), food caches, communal fire rings and pit toilets. Some beautiful old-growth trees tower above the junction of the side trail to Eric Lake. The early settlers had difficulty getting around Eric Lake and used the lake itself as a transportation corridor to access San Josef Bay. The original road from Fisherman River thus ended at the northern end of the lake. You will encounter vestiges of this old road as you walk towards Fisherman River. You will also be able to spot the remains of an old telegraph line and later some old fence posts along the trail. This portion of the trail closely parallels St. Mary Creek, which eventually empties into the Fisherman River. Recently a small camping area, consisting of two tent platforms, was established at a site just past the bridge over the Fisherman River. There is also an outhouse here. A food cache will be installed in the future.

If you are determined and got off to an early start, it is possible with decent weather to make it from the trailhead to one of the two premier beach camping areas in the park: Nissen Bight or Nels Bight. About 3 kilometers (2 miles) after you cross the Fisherman River you will come to an intersection. The right fork takes you down a muddy and at times slippery clay path for approximately 2 kilometers (1.2 miles) to Nissen Bight. The left fork goes to the north part of Hansen Lagoon and then through the trees to Nels Bight. Just before you reach this intersection there is a small side path to your right that leads to the grave marker of William Christensen, the other adopted son of Carl Brink Christensen, who died at the age of twelve. He cut his foot and died from blood poisoning for lack of medical care. His gravestone is an impressive pillar of pink granite about 1.7 meters (6 feet) high.

Nissen Bight is more secluded and visited less than Nels Bight. There is good beach camping on sand, and water is available from a creek at the east end of the beach. Pit toilets and food caches are also present. At low tide it is possible to explore around the point to the

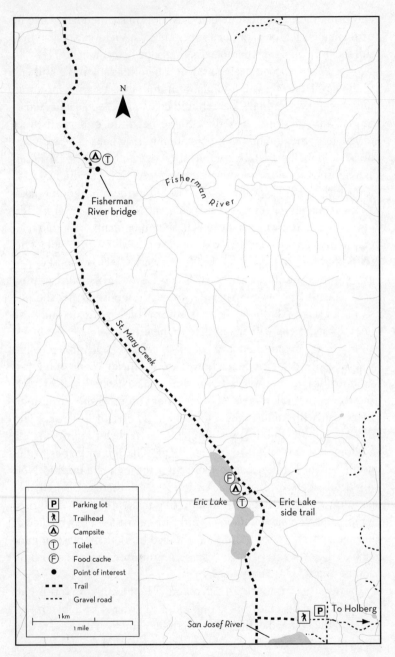

MAP 16: CAPE SCOTT TRAIL—ERIC LAKE TO FISHERMAN RIVER

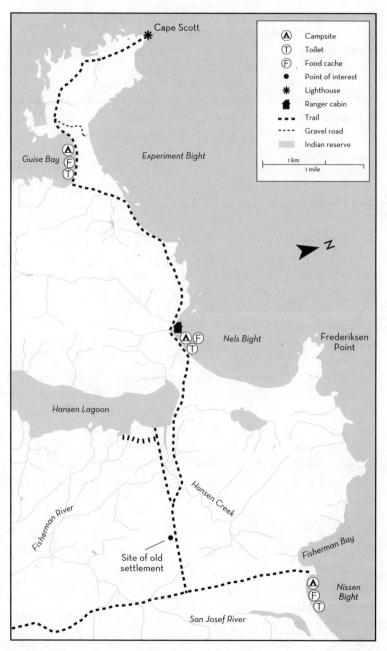

MAP 17: CAPE SCOTT TRAIL—FISHERMAN RIVER TO CAPE SCOTT

west and walk into Fisherman Bay. This is the site of the first disembarkation by the early Danish colonists. For years this was the place where the monthly steamer arrived with supplies and news from the outside world.

If your destination is Nels Bight, then you have another 1.5 hours' walking from the junction to the beach. However, allow some time to explore, since you will be traveling past many of the remnants of the settlement. Information boards erected by BC Parks tell some of the story of this area. One of the last larger farms belonged to Alfred Spencer, who left in 1956. As you walk to the west, you will be traversing the north end of the grassy fields that were diked by the settlers. It is possible to continue along this path and arrive at Hansen Lagoon. The area around here was diked in two stages. The part at the northeastern edge of the lagoon was finished in 1905. If you turn to the south, you can hike along the lagoon's edge to view the site of the original dike, constructed of rocks in 1899. The lagoon is on the Pacific flyway for many migrating shorebirds and waterfowl and is a good spot for birdwatching.

If you want a respite from that weight on your back, turn to your right about 1 kilometer (0.6 mile) past the Nissen/Nels junction and descend through a forested area to the beach. This is the camping mecca for most hikers, and oftentimes there will be twenty to thirty tents billowing in the breeze along the strand here. Food caches and toilets are located at the west end of this beach. The best water source is the stream that enters the beach near there. A ranger cabin is located on the far side of this creek. Many visitors stay at Nels and use it as a base camp for exploring the cape area farther to the west. One problem that has been reported from campers at Nels is severe burns caused by walking on or uncovering buried fire sites. If you have a beach fire, ensure that it is extinguished with water and not simply buried with sand.

If you want to avoid the tanning crowd and you like beautiful spots, then shoulder your load for Guise Bay, one of the most exquisite places on the planet (when it is sunny). To get there take the trail out of Nels past the ranger cabin and hike overland to Experiment Bight. You can walk along the beach here until you reach an old plank road. This was constructed during World War II to link up

Sand neck, Guise Bay, PHOTO BY A. DORST

some buildings from that era that have now descended into ruins.
Follow this plank road south across the sand neck to arrive at Guise
Bay. The usual accoutrements of camping (caches, toilets) await
you. A water source is present on the east end of the beach in the
form of a small stream.

The sand neck was the site of an attempt by one of the Danish
colonists, N.P. Jensen, to stabilize the shifting sand dunes through
construction of a driftwood fence. You may still see remnants of the
original fence that runs east-west in some places. This place was also
well known among the First Nations groups. Several battles between
warring First Nations were fought here. At the west end of the beach
at Experiment Bight, you can still see the remains of a midden, a

Black-tailed deer

concentration of shell and bone fragments that denotes a site used by First Nations people.

If your destination is Cape Scott Lighthouse, then from Guise Bay take the path at the west end of the beach. A road that services the lighthouse leads up from the beach and eventually ends at the lighthouse proper. The lighthouse is near the cape itself. Formerly it was possible to hike out to the cape over a suspension bridge and up and down countless stairs. However, the Canadian government closed and later dismantled these structures for fear of liability issues arising from hikers using them. Please note that the lighthouse and surrounding area are not part of the park.

Cape Scott Provincial Park was increased in size in 1995 through the creation of the Nahwitti-Shushartie corridor. The plan is to construct a trail called the North Coast Trail that connects Cape Scott with Shushartie Bay 47 kilometers (29 miles) to the east. This pathway would follow the early route of the settlers; remains of an old road connect the settlement near Fisherman Bay to Shushartie Bay. This addition is expected to be completed within a few years and will add a 47-kilometer (29-mile) long trail to the park. It is expected that the trail will cross two major rivers, the Nahwitti and Shushartie, via suspension bridges.

> ## OTHER AREAS OF INTEREST

If you have a few extra days to add to a visit to Cape Scott Provincial Park, there are some other areas you may enjoy visiting. Raft Cove Provincial Park is within an easy drive of Cape Scott and offers some beautiful beach walking that is not as crowded as the bights at Cape Scott.

> ### *Raft Cove*
DISTANCE: 1.5 km (0.9 mile) · TIME: 45–60 minutes · RATING: 3 E I
Very rough trail

> ### *Ronning Gardens*
DISTANCE: 0.5 km (0.3 mile) · TIME: 15–20 minutes · RATING: 1 B
Easy trail to private gardens. Recommended

> ## RAFT COVE PROVINCIAL PARK

To reach Raft Cove Provincial Park, turn left at the junction of San Josef Main and Ronning Main and follow the signs for Raft Cove Provincial Park and Cape Palmerston recreation area. There is a very small parking area (space for four to five cars) at the end of a 1-kilometer (0.6-mile) narrow road that leads off Ronning Mainline. The first third of the trail at present is in very rough condition. (BC Parks advise that it has plans to improve portions of the trail.) After you descend a small hill from the parking lot, you will meet your first major obstacle. A small creek drains in from your left with a very tricky log crossing. If the trail has received a fair share of rain recently, the creek will be high and will flood an area adjacent to this crossing, making the approach to the log somewhat difficult. Past this point there are several large quagmires to circumnavigate or plunge through, depending on the depth of the mud. Probe with a staff or hiking pole before you wade in.

As the trail begins to gain elevation, the obstacles and mud will decrease. However, there are still a few slippery logs to negotiate. When you reach a noticeable height of land, you will arrive at a fork in the trail and should be able to hear the surf below you. Follow the trail to your left at this juncture over a large downed cedar. The trail is well marked with orange tape. The trail to your right leads straight down to the coast. Marked with white and some orange tape, it will take you out to a headland. If the tide is high, you will have some difficulty getting onto the beach from this headland. The left fork leads down to the north end of the beach. From here it is a pleasant beach walk to the Macjack River, where most of the protected campsites are located.

As you proceed to the Macjack, you will pass a small stream within the first 200 meters (650 feet). The water here is potable after treatment and is better than the brackish water of the Macjack. There are pit toilets, and a signed food cache is located just off the beach, on the peninsula of land framed by the Macjack River. Raft Cove has a beautiful sandy beach about 1 kilometer (0.6 mile) long. It affords good surfing, and there is good fishing in season in the river. At low tide and low flows you can ford the river inland from its mouth. Take care in crossing. On the opposite side of the river are the remains of the Hecht cabin. Willie Hecht first moved here in 1913. He was one of the last settlers from the two waves of settlers into the area to leave.

According to the official management plan for the park, future plans include vehicle access to the beach along with a large drive-in campground.

> ## CAPE PALMERSTON RECREATION AREA

The Cape Palmerston recreation area is located about 10 minutes' drive from Raft Cove Provincial Park. Although there is limited hiking in this area, the beach is accessible in 5 minutes of easy walking

Ronning Gardens

from the parking lot. Once on the beach you can explore the rocky headlands in both directions from your campsite. Cape Palmerston was named after Lord Henry Palmerston, a prime minister of Britain during the nineteenth century.

To reach this area, continue along Ronning Mainline and follow the signs past the turnoff to Raft Cove. There is a good-sized parking area located just before you reach a short trail that takes you past some pit toilets to the beach area. The beach here, which consists of small pebbles, is readily accessible but has limited spots for good camping. A creek drains out to the south and can be easily forded at low tides and low water flows. It is possible to hike around the headland to your south for a few kilometers to an emergency cabin.

> ## RONNING GARDENS

En route to Cape Scott Provincial Park you will pass a sign on the road about 1 kilometer (0.6 mile) past the intersection of Ronning Mainline and San Josef Mainline logging roads. A few meters past the sign is a short road that takes you to a parking area. Park here and walk west along an easy path that is the old wagon road that linked the settlements of San Josef Bay and Holberg. It takes about 10 to 15 minutes to reach the gardens.

Bernt Ronning was a Norwegian immigrant who settled in this area in 1910 and remained until the 1960s. His garden was renowned for the exotic species of plants that he collected and replanted here. Two large monkey-puzzle trees flank the entrance to the garden. The current owners collect the seeds from these trees and grow them into seedlings in a small nursery on-site. An information board near the entrance provides a brief history of Ronning and the gardens. The current owners do not charge a fee for visiting but accept contributions towards the upkeep of the grounds.

Although Cape Scott is remote, accessible along rough logging roads and notoriously wet, it is highly recommended as a hiking destination. The place has a mystical feel to it, and the old-growth forests provide welcome respite from the harried lifestyles that many of us lead.

8

NATURAL
HISTORY

· · · · ·

All of British Columbia has been mapped into biogeoclimatic zones. Vladimir Krajina, a Czech botanist who immigrated to Canada and taught at the University of British Columbia for many years, developed this concept. The theory is that plants can be grouped (especially tree or grass species) on the basis of soil characteristics and weather patterns. By taking many samples from diverse ecosystems across the province, Krajina and his students were able to define from an ecosystem perspective the whole landmass of the province. This immense undertaking has contributed to an ability to predict the natural history of areas. The development of this system has also enabled the setting aside of ecological reserves and protected areas that preserve distinct biogeoclimatic zones.

Western Vancouver Island is included within the Coastal Western Hemlock (CWH) biogeoclimatic zone. A layperson would call this area a rain forest, and such a zone is noted for its high rate of productivity. Soils are rich in humus and full of nutrients, so plants thrive on the organic compost-like material. The limiting factor for growth in such an environment is usually sunlight.

Four main species of large conifers are commonly found along the hikes described in this book: Douglas-fir, western hemlock, western red cedar and Sitka spruce. These trees, which thrive on the west coast of Vancouver Island, grow to enormous size and are long-lived; some are as much as a thousand years old. Douglas-fir, *Pseudotsuga menziesii*, is generally found in younger, more open forests than the other species. This species is distinguished by cones with three-pronged bracts and has thick, ridged bark. Sitka spruce, *Picea*

Sea lions off the Juan de Fuca Marine Trail, PHOTO BY A. DORST

sitchensis, is found along the coast and up some of the valleys, such as the Carmanah and Walbran valleys. This species has scaly bark and very sharp needles. If you grab onto a branch and the needles dig into the skin of your palm, chances are good that you have hold of a Sitka spruce. The boughs of this tree were used in ceremonial dances by the Nuu-chah-nulth to ward off evil spirits. Spruce is tolerant of salt water and is thus found close to the shoreline.

Away from the exposed coast, western hemlock, *Tsuga heterophylla*, and western red cedar, *Thuja plicata*, are the dominant species. Hemlock is distinguished by a drooping crown with graceful boughs, flat small needles and relatively smooth bark. This species tolerates shade and will grow beneath other species of trees. Cedar has ropy reddish-brown bark. It is perhaps the most important tree in the coastal Native culture and is the official tree of British Columbia. First Nations people used the wood for longhouses and totem poles. They also used many other parts of the tree. Seedlings are tolerant of shade and are found in the understory of mature forests. Cedar burns well even when wet and is quite aromatic.

You will find the occasional shore pine, *Pinus contorta*, along the coast in areas that lack groundwater. In young forests, such as the one west of Sombrio River, you will find deciduous species of trees, especially red alder, *Alnus rubra*, and vine maple, *Acer circinatum*.

The understory of the rain forest is too diverse to describe here. It is thickest in the open areas and sparser in the dark, mature forest. Salal, *Gaultheria shallon*, is the most common west coast shrub; it ranges from low ground cover to impenetrable jungle, sometimes growing to a height of 2.5 meters (more than 8 feet). Salmonberry, *Rubus spectabilis*, is thick in many areas, and its berries (red when ripe; salmon-colored or orange when not) will provide a quick snack along many of the paths. Other edible berries in this area include huckleberry (*Vaccinium* spp.), thimbleberry (*Rubus parviflorus*) and wild blackberry (*Rubus ursinus*). Numerous ferns are found in shaded, damp forest and along the moist banks of streams.

In the bogs you will find a diversity of plant species quite different from the ones found in the rain forest. Of particular interest are the insectivorous plants such as the sundew (*Drosera rotundifolia*). Trees are usually stunted because of the nutrient-poor environment. Shore pine and yellow-cedar (*Chamaecyparis nootkatensis*) are commonly found in these areas. Peat mosses (*Sphagnum* spp.) and other species of moss also abound in this wet zone. The mosses often form small hummocks or tussocks. Along the coast, a great variety of seaweed is visible in the ocean at low tide. One remarkable species is the sea palm, *Postelsia*, which clings to the rocks at the most turbulent part of the low-tide zone. It is an impressive sight to watch the sea palm bend under the impact of huge breakers and then spring back intact after the wave has passed. There are too many plants and animals within the intertidal zone to discuss here. Take along a good guidebook if you are interested in the fascinating life of a tide pool. Several such books are listed at the back of this book.

Not many large animals are spotted along the coast trails, since the forest is usually so dense. Black-tailed deer (*Odocoileus hemionus*), black bear (*Ursus americanus*), cougar (*Felis concolor*) and wolf (*Canis lupus*) are sometimes sighted, however. Both California and Steller's sea lions are found offshore along the coast. Steller's sea lions (*Eumetopias jubata*) are more commonly spotted—they are generally larger and blonder than the California sea lion (*Zalophus californianus*) and growl rather than bark. Sea lions are best spotted near the Pachena Point and Carmanah Point lighthouses offshore on rocky islets. Harbour seals (*Phoca vitulina*) and river otters (*Lutra canadensis*) are commonly observed along the the southwest coast of the island.

Sea otters (*Enhydra lutris*) are gradually making a comeback from the devastating fur trade of the nineteenth century that nearly eradicated the species. They may be found along the coast from east of Cape Scott as far south as Estevan Point. The principal diet of sea otters are red sea urchins (*Strongylocentrotus franciscanus*). Where the sea otter has been eliminated, the red sea urchin has grown exponentially. Urchins eat prodigious amounts of algae and create desert-like areas on the seabed known as urchin barrens. Where sea otters have been re-established, the populations of urchins are kept in check and the large kelp beds along the coast are coming back. One can readily see evidence of this when hiking the Nootka Trail near Bajo and Maquinna points.

During the summer months, feeding gray whales (*Eschrictius robustus*) are often espied from shore. Look for the tell-tale spout

Moon snail shell, Whitesand Cove, Flores Island

that indicates a whale is offshore. Good areas for whale spotting are along the West Coast Trail from Darling River to Klanawa River, at Ahous Bay on Vargas Island, at Cow Bay on Flores Island and from Third Beach to Calvin Falls on Nootka Island.

Small mammals such as red squirrel *(Tamiasciurus hudsonicus)*, raccoon *(Procyon lotor)* and mink *(Mustela vison)* are more abundant than the larger ones. Several types of mice frequent camping spots. You may discover signs of their presence if you leave food in your pack rather than in a food cache up a tree.

Bird life is rich; bald eagles *(Haliaeetus leucocephalus)* are common, as are aquatic and marine species of birds such as loons,

Nootka Trail

mergansers and gulls. The marbled murrelet (*Brachyramphus marmoratus*) has become a symbol of the Carmanah Valley since a nest was first discovered there. This small sea bird fishes by day in the ocean and returns to nest in the high branches of tall trees in the old-growth forest. With the increasing disappearance of its nesting habitat, the marbled murrelet has become rare. If you are an avid bird watcher, Parks Canada produces a handy checklist of the more than 250 species of birds that may be spotted in Pacific Rim National Park Reserve.

There are a number of salmon spawning runs in the streams along the coast. Sockeye, chum and coho salmon (*Oncorhynchus* spp.) spawn in Hobiton Lake, which is reached via the Nitinat Narrows. The fish in this creek-lake system spawn in gravel along the perimeter of Hobiton Lake rather than in the streambed. If you are in this area in the fall, take care when choosing your campsite. The sockeye in the Cheewhat River system are unusual because the spawners return throughout the year rather than at one time. This was an important factor for the First Nations who settled the area. The chum salmon fishery of the Doobah River, which flows into Nitinat Lake, was once the richest along the coast. Through a combination of overfishing and improper logging practices, the salmon were eliminated from this river. The same pattern has been repeated for many of the streams along the coast; particularly hard hit have been the chinook and coho salmon species. Recently wild salmon have had to compete with escapees from fish farms. Many of the fish farms breed Atlantic salmon, which are not endemic to the area. These stocks potentially can affect the wild populations, since fish kept in close quarters tend to develop bacteria and viral infections. Fish farmers provide antibiotics to the fish with their feed. However, wild salmon stocks are not inoculated against these diseases.

The taking or disturbing of wildlife is expressly prohibited in any of the parks described in this guide. This ban applies to all shellfish, including mussels and crab. All living creatures and plants as well as their fossilized remains are forbidden to be removed.

During the summer a phenomenon known as red tide may occur. Eating filter-feeding molluscs and shellfish during a red tide can result in a potentially fatal disease called paralytic shellfish poisoning

(PSP). Watch for notices at the Information Centres at the West Coast Trail or Juan de Fuca trailheads about shellfish closures in the area. Visit the Fisheries and Oceans Web site (www.dfo-mpo.gc.ca) for up-to-date information on red tide and shellfish closures.

Some of the animals you may see are becoming increasingly rare. Sea otters and the marbled murrelet, for example, are red-listed by the British Columbia Conservation Data Centre. This means that they are one step away from being placed on the threatened or endangered list, where the extirpation of the species is a real and imminent prospect. The step before red-listing a species is blue-listing. Species such as the tufted puffin and gray whale are in this latter category. Generally these species are still considered to be at risk, though not as high at risk as the red-listed ones.

Keep in mind that the wild creatures in these areas inhabited the wilderness long before humans. Many hikers want to see these creatures in their unspoiled natural habitat. Keep your disturbance of the landscape to a minimum and you will help to guarantee that these species continue to reside here for many years.

9

FIRST

NATIONS

· · · · ·

At the time of contact with Europeans in 1778, two main groups of
aboriginal people inhabited the west coast of Vancouver Island.
Members of the Kwakwaka'wakw lived in the north part of the
island, and the Nuu-chah-nulth (formerly and erroneously called
Nootka) lived on the central and southern coast. The Nuu-chah-
nulth were famed canoe builders. They carved the large cedar trees
that are found in the rain forest into seagoing canoes for pursuing
whales and halibut. Of all the Northwest Coast groups of aborigi-
nals, only the Nuu-chah-nulth ventured far out to sea in pursuit
of gray and humpback whales. The name Nuu-chah-nulth means
"all along the mountains," which refers to the image of their homeland when they were returning to Vancouver Island after being far
out at sea.

Today there are three separate First Nations whose traditional
homeland is the southwest coast of Vancouver Island. The
Pacheedaht reside near Port Renfrew, the Ditidaht in the Nitinat
Lake area and the Huu-ay-aht at Pachena Bay and Cape Beale. All
three groups belong to the Nuu-chah-nulth language group, which
is divided into three linguistic subdivisions: the northern and central
groups speak dialects of one language, while the Ditidaht are linguis-
tically more related to the Makah of the Olympic Peninsula. The
Ditidaht and Pacheedaht First Nations speak a similar dialect,
whereas the Huu-ay-aht are more closely related to the northern
Nuu-chah-nulth groups. Pacheedaht means "children of the sea
foam"; these people used to travel far out to the Swiftsure Banks
from Cullite Cove to catch halibut.

Totem Pole, Yuquot

These three groups have reserve lands along the West Coast Trail and in the Nitinat Triangle portion of Pacific Rim National Park and Reserve. The reserve lands near Port Renfrew, Clo-oose, Whyac, the Hobiton River, the Ditidaht village on Nitinat Lake and Pachena Bay are all inhabited. Other reserve lands are uninhabited. All reserve lands are clearly marked on the maps of the area. They are private lands, and no trespassing is permitted even if they are unoccupied. Although portions of the trail may pass through a reserve, you must remain on the trail. No camping or removal of wood is allowed unless you have the consent of members of the First Nation.

The West Coast Trail is patrolled by guardians of the Quu'as. Quu'as personnel come from the three First Nations and provide services such as ferry crossings at Nitinat Narrows and the Gordon River. They are also engaged in orientation for hikers, trail repair and maintenance, and protection of cultural resources. Cabins that house Quu'as guardians are located near Tsocowis Creek, Tsuquadra Creek and Camper Bay. Do not bother the staff unless you have an emergency or wish to report a serious problem with the condition of the trail.

Several bands of First Nations reside along the central coast of Vancouver Island. In the Long Beach area there are the Ucluelet and Tla-o-qui-aht (formerly known as the Clayoquot) peoples. Farther to the north, on Flores and Vargas islands, live the Ahousaht. The Hesquiaht inhabit areas in the vicinity of Estevan Point and the Mowachaht, the "people of the deer," reside on Nootka Island. In pre-contact times, these Nuu-chah-nulth peoples lived through a seasonal migration pattern. During the spring and summer they would move out close to the coast and harvest the rich shellfish and animal life that is found there. In the autumn they would head inland to take advantage of the salmon runs in some of the area's streams and rivers. They would overwinter inland in their permanent village sites to escape the winter storms that are prevalent along the coast.

The Kwakwaka'wakw dwelled in the north part of the island at the time of European contact. This linguistic group is related to the First Nations of the northern coast of British Columbia around Bella Bella. The Kwakwaka'wakw were known for their elaborate ceremonies and potlatch system. Potlatches are elaborate gift-giving feasts and ceremonies that were prevalent among the coastal aboriginal peoples. They represent a form of gift economy where leadership and hierarchy are established through redistribution of wealth. Beautifully carved masks were used in many of their ceremonies. From 1884 until 1954, the Canadian government prohibited potlatches, even though they formed part of the inherent culture of the coastal First Nations.

Two groups of First Nations claim the Cape Scott area as being within their traditional territory: the Tlatlasikwala First Nation on Hope Island and the Quatsino, who reside further south. The Tlatlasikwala were formerly known as the Nahwitti. They were allocated some Indian reserves now within the confines of Cape Scott Provincial Park.

As was the case for many First Nations, contact with Europeans brought diseases that had devastating effect upon the Native populations of Vancouver Island. The Yutlinuk who inhabited the Cape Scott Islands died out in the early 1800s.

All of the First Nations in the area covered by the trails in this book are involved in treaty negotiations with the Canadian and British Columbia governments. At stake are large tracts of land being claimed as traditional lands by the First Nations in order to protect their traditional ways of hunting and fishing. The Quu'as program on the West Coast Trail and the Wild Side Trail on Flores Island are examples of how First Nations work with conservationists and outdoor groups to improve the quality of the hiking experience.

10

CONSERVATION

. . . . .

People who live on islands quickly become aware that land is limited. The competition for the land and its fruits, particularly timber, has driven the history of conservation efforts on Vancouver Island. Over the years logging interests have been given permission to harvest much of the old-growth timber on the southern and eastern coasts of the island. The right to harvest much of the timber on the island's west coast has similarly been granted by the province. Lands set aside as parklands or ecological reserves are all people now have available to them in which to hike or explore the wilderness. One could very well ask how we got into this situation. To answer that query, it becomes important to trace the history of land use on the west coast of Vancouver Island.

In the 1950s, when Chief Justice Gordon Sloan chaired two royal commissions of inquiry into the forest industry, his main conclusion was that Crown forests should be managed to allow sustained yield. To implement this program, the B.C. Forest Service, as it was then known, which lacked the finances and staff to directly administer all of the Crown forest land, established many areas as Tree Farm Licenses (TFLs), which were then leased to major logging companies. In this way, much of the forested Crown land on Vancouver Island was committed to logging; and, since tourism was not yet developed to the point of making significant contribution to the economy of the province, very little attention was paid to future recreational and preservationist needs.

Once the TFLs were created, the parks system then in existence on Vancouver Island was all the recreational land the public had

Flores Island, PHOTO BY A. DORST

access to, unless the government was prepared to preserve areas committed to logging. When the province in subsequent governments made a commitment to conserve wilderness values through setting aside land for such a purpose, the major logging companies sought compensation for removal of timber from their TFLs and other forestry-based tenures.

The history of the conservation efforts to preserve the West Coast Trail and the Nitinat Triangle exemplifies a classic struggle over land use. When the Pacific Rim National Park was created in 1969, the boundaries of the trail were provisionally set as a kilometer-wide (0.6-mile-wide) strip except for enlargements at Cape Beale and Clo-oose. These narrow boundaries omitted the Nitinat Lake area, which held exceptional recreation potential and scientific interest.

Other attractive areas, such as Black Lake and the Klanawa Valley, were also omitted. In 1970, the Canadian National Parks Branch requested that the Province of B.C. include the Nitinat Triangle in the proposed national park. The Province, prodded by the logging companies, which held the TFLs in the area, balked. This was the beginning of the local conflict between logging companies and conservationists.

In the years between 1970 and 1992, when the West Coast Trail and Nitinat Lake officially became part of Pacific Rim National Park Reserve, much discussion and negotiation took place over compensation to the logging companies by way of land trades. The difficulty has always been finding suitable land bases on Vancouver Island to trade to the major companies for loss of cutting rights. Those trades were eventually made, and private land holdings around Clo-oose were relinquished to the Crown and are now part of the national park.

After the struggle to have the West Coast Trail and the Nitinat Lake area set aside as parkland had been resolved, the conservation focus on southern Vancouver Island shifted to the Carmanah and Walbran watersheds. In theory a watershed represents a complete ecosystem. Although certain components of such an ecosystem may range outside the watershed's boundaries, for the most part the plant species and smaller creatures form a cohesive system. Environmentalists as well as ecologists and scientists recognized the need to preserve some of the original, mature old-growth watersheds on the west coast of the Island. These forests have evolved over centuries, and many groups and individuals wanted them to be preserved before they were forever lost to the corporate interests of the logging companies that held the rights to the timber.

In the early 1990s public interest focused upon saving some of the large coastal trees that are found in old-growth forests. Due to the efforts of conservationists, the lower Carmanah Valley was set aside as a provincial park. Then the discovery of the first marbled murrelet nest in Canada in the Walbran Valley galvanized efforts by environmental groups to include the upper Carmanah and Walbran valleys as parkland. In 1995 these efforts were rewarded through the creation of the Carmanah Walbran Provincial Park, which contains two wholly protected watersheds within its confines: Logan and Cullite creeks. Yet compared with the former old-growth paradise of the entire west coast of Vancouver Island, the land base preserved as old-growth forest today is paltry.

Disputes such as those in the Walbran and Carmanah valleys often come down to a question of the "best" economic use of land. Tourism and recreation needs on southwestern Vancouver Island have outpaced the increasing demands of the logging companies for timber. The very fact that Pacific Rim National Park Reserve instituted a much-needed quota system in the 1990s to limit the number of hikers on the West Coast Trail is evidence that the recreational demand in this area has far outstripped the availability of similar wilderness experiences.

In contrast to an economy based upon timber harvesting, if the forests were available for use by scientists, recreational users and conservationists, their value could be spread out over several generations in perpetuity. More than ten thousand people are drawn just to the West Coast Trail each year. These people contribute to the economies of Port Renfrew, Port Alberni and Bamfield, with various spinoff effects on the rest of southern Vancouver Island. When the *long-term* economic effects of tourism and recreational use of the old-growth forests on southern Vancouver Island are compared with the economic effects of logging, it is clear that preserving the forests is much more economically viable than clear-cutting them.

Moreover, we are only just beginning to grasp the relationship between the disappearance of old growth and the dwindling numbers of salmon. Although the issue of reduced salmon populations is complicated by other demands on the fish, including international disputes that may lead to overfishing and dangers to wild stocks posed by fish farms, one of the recognized reasons for their decline is habitat destruction. Work underway on the central coast of British Columbia aims to describe the complicated natural system that connects salmon, bears and forests.

Meanwhile, the demand for wilderness experience on southern Vancouver Island has increased even as the hectares of remaining old-growth forest have decreased. An increase in tourism can create problems in wilderness overuse, requiring measures such as the quota system for the West Coast Trail. To reduce this pressure, areas

Lismer Beach, Pacific Rim National Park

Pachena Bay, West Coast Trail

in addition to the West Coast Trail have been set aside. The creation of the Juan de Fuca Trail and the Carmanah Walbran Provincial Park plus additions to Cape Scott Provincial Park and the new North Coast Trail that is currently being developed will help in the short term. But what happens when these areas too become crowded? The wilderness experience that is a recognized need of the human soul may become harder to find.

To appreciate the effect of logging on an old-growth forest, it is important to understand the forest's history and the changes that would be brought about if it were logged. In the coastal western hemlock biogeoclimatic zone, the forest moves through several transitions, known as stages of succession, before it reaches its climax state, when it can reproduce itself. After a major fire (or clear-cut logging), the first species to recolonize the land are usually fireweed, shrubs and alder. These pioneer species are in great abundance on the Juan de Fuca Trail in the vicinity of Parkinson Creek. The pioneer stage is followed by Douglas-fir, which cannot regenerate in shade. As the Douglas-fir forest ages and dies, it is replaced by a cedar-hemlock forest, which regenerates itself, since the seedlings of these species are able to tolerate shade. A western hemlock and western red cedar forest is thus the climax forest of the west coast of southern Vancouver Island. A Douglas-fir forest is considered to be temporary. Along most of the eastern coast of Vancouver Island, fires have historically prevented the forest from reaching a climax stage. Logging now performs that same function in most parts of British Columbia outside of parkland. But on the island's west coast and in some of its valleys, fires are rare because of high rainfall, and many forests have evolved for thousands of years without interference.

Thus, the climax forest is a multi-age forest, which may have taken up to two thousand years to evolve. This forest is characterized by enormous trees, limited undergrowth (which makes travel relatively easy) and a forest floor rich in small plants, mosses, ferns, lichens and many unusual fungi. Such a forest is often described as "decadent" or "overmature" by industrial foresters, because older trees grow slowly and contain a high proportion of rot. But such a forest also provides critical habitat for endangered species of wildlife such as spotted owls, marbled murrelets and spotted salamanders.

The replacement forest in a clear-cut has an entirely different character. For the first twenty years it is virtually impenetrable as the young trees grow. The bush tends to be thick salal, and berries such as salmonberry and blackberry abound. For the next twenty years the forest stand is still full of logging debris and the dead young trees crowded out by competition with their neighbors. The richness of the forest floor is gone, logging debris impedes travel and wildlife habitat is destroyed. Only in the last half of the cycle does the forest become attractive to the hiker. But the gigantic trees are gone forever.

Clear-cut logging also alters water quality and hydrodynamics. Without the large trees and their enormous root systems to hold the soil, topsoil is easily eroded by the rains and is washed out to sea. Along the way streams become filled with silt, and salmon habitat and spawning beds are destroyed. Incessant winter rains erode the rich humus needed to replenish life in the forest. Loss of humus not only makes it more difficult for trees to regenerate but also means that fewer nutrients are available to the entire ecosystem.

Graphic examples of clear-cut logging are all too evident on southern Vancouver Island. Along the way to the trailheads at Port Renfrew, Bamfield, the Carmanah Walbran and Cape Scott, extensive clear-cuts can be seen from the road—in stark contrast to the lush old-growth forests you enter once you begin to hike.

British Columbia is advertised as a tourist's paradise. Every year visitors flock here from many countries that have already logged their forests and destroyed their wilderness. Tourists want to see the exceptional. The old climax forests of the Nitinat Triangle, along the West Coast Trail and in the Carmanah and Walbran valleys *are* exceptional—uniform second-growth stands are not.

Ecosystem-based land management (often abbreviated to EBM) is just beginning to be realized and implemented. Too often in the past, government planners based park boundaries upon arbitrary or humanly defined aspects. Wild creatures cannot read maps and will wander where they will. Many creatures need sufficient territory in order simply to survive. Preserving entire watersheds is often necessary to preserve entire ecosystems. However, for many of the hikes described in this book, what has been set aside is a simple hiking corridor. Therefore, instead of ecosystems, there are strips of land along the coast that are preserved for hiking or recreational pursuits. These strips vary in width, averaging just under a kilometer (about half a mile) for trails such as the West Coast Trail. This width is not sufficient to prevent the encroachment of preserved areas by logging roads.

In addition, when the timber companies have done their work, one of the inevitable results of leaving a clear-cut zone behind a narrow strip of forest is to create a blowdown effect. The heavy sea winds rush into the vacuum created by the clear-cut and push over the trees standing in the way. Evidence of this blowdown effect can be seen between Camper Bay and Sandstone Creek on the West Coast Trail, and on the Juan de Fuca Trail between Payzant Creek and Sombrio River. In contrast, the corridor allotted to the beach

Schooner Cove, Pacific Rim National Park

trail at Olympic National Park in Washington averages 5 kilometers (3 miles) in width.

The one trail listed in this book that is not yet protected in any long-term fashion is the Nootka Trail, on Nootka Island. The provincial Ministry of Sustainable Resource Management is responsible for land use planning. They have produced a plan for the coastal area of Nootka Island, which may be found on-line at srmwww.gov.bc.ca/rmd/coastal/north_island/nootka. Although this plan takes into consideration the recreational value of the Nootka Trail, it does not actually protect any of the land bases of the trail itself. The plan is also deficient in that the corridor set aside for the trail is too narrow. The government might have benefited from lessons learned on the West Coast Trail concerning blowdowns, but this does not appear to be the case. The present plan calls for a corridor of a mere 200 meters (650 feet). This is grossly insufficient. In addition, the first part of the trail, from Louie Lagoon to Third Beach, is left unprotected. The

Nuu-chah-nulth Trail, Pacific Rim National Park

beautiful forested hill that dominates the view to the southeast from Third Beach is also not preserved under the proposed plan. In 2004 more than one thousand hikers visited Nootka Island to marvel at the unspoiled beauty of the remote west coast. Surely that number should have some impact on those who do the planning and who have the power to set aside such land.

BC Parks went through, and in some cases is still going through, a process to develop master plans for provincial park usages. These plans form the basis for future decisions on anything from allowing lodges in parks to permitting logging and mining within park boundaries. The provincial government's current philosophy is that parks ought to be able to pay for themselves. This concept does not bode well for the recreational user or, for that matter, the wildlife within the park itself. If you are interested in learning more about provincial parks, most of the planning information is available on the BC Parks Web site, wlapwww.gov.bc.ca/bcparks.

Even the oceans off the shores of British Columbia are not necessarily as sacrosanct as they once were. Recently the provincial government has been lobbying the federal government to lift the moratoria on oil exploration along the B.C. coast. The Tofino Basin is offshore of the central west coast of Vancouver Island; it is believed to hold large amounts of fossil fuels. Although it is too early to predict whether and where oil platforms will be erected and where or how the oil and gas will be transported to refineries, conservationists are concerned that there be strict environmental controls over exploratory drilling and development of these resources. If not, we face potential loss of wildlife and pollution of our pristine beaches similar to that experienced on too many coasts on too many occasions around the world when there has been an oil spill either from a tanker or a drilling platform.

Conservationists in British Columbia must be vigilant to ensure that no encroachment of existing wilderness occurs. They must also continue to act to help set aside additional public lands for wilderness, scientific, ecological and recreational values. If these wilderness areas and old-growth forests are clear-cut, not only British Columbia but also the rest of the world will lose a valuable resource. You need only to hike along the coastal trails or visit the giant trees in the

Carmanah Valley to understand that these places are indeed sacred and ought to be preserved.

This book has been written to help hikers enjoy the west coast of Vancouver Island and to appreciate that wilderness is a priceless and endangered resource. Everyone who has hiked even a few kilometers of the trails described in this book has experienced the natural beauty of the area. If those thousands of hikers were moved to voice their support for wilderness, writing e-mails and letters to the provincial and federal governments urging that further wilderness areas be preserved, then the wilderness message of the West Coast Trail and environs may have its most profound effect. Your views are important and ought to be made known to the politicians responsible for deciding the future of British Columbia's wilderness.

The following URLs are provided so that you may obtain information from governments on their policies and the names of ministries responsible for parks, land use and forestry in B.C.

> www.gov.bc.ca
This is the home page for the Province of British Columbia, which contains links to the various provincial government departments.

> canada.gc.ca
This is the main page for the Government of Canada.

FOR FURTHER
READING

· · · · ·

Abraham, Dorothy. *Lone Cone: A Journal of Life on the West Coast of Vancouver Island.* Victoria: privately published, 1961.

Akrigg, G.P.V., and Helen Akrigg. *British Columbia Place Names.* 3rd ed. Victoria: Sono Nis Press, 1986. (reprinted by University of British Columbia Press 1997)

Blier, Richard K. *Hiking Trails III, Central and Northern Vancouver Island.* 9th ed. Victoria: Vancouver Island Trail Information Society, 2002.

Cannings, Richard J. and Sydney G. Cannings. *British Columbia: A Natural History.* Vancouver: Greystone Books, 1996.

Clutesi, George. *Potlatch.* Sidney: Gray's Publishing Ltd., 1969.

George, Chief Earl Maquinna. *Living on the Edge, Nuu-Chah-Nulth History from an Ahousaht Chief's Perspective.* Winlaw: Sono Nis Press, 2003.

Gill, Ian. *Hiking on the Edge.* Vancouver: Raincoast Books, 1995.

Godman, Josephine E. *Pioneer Days of Port Renfrew.* Victoria: Solitaire Publishing, 1973.

Horvath, Pal. *The Nootka Trail: A Backpacker's Guide.* 2nd ed. Campbell River, B.C.: Ptarmigan Press, 2004.

Jewitt, John R. *White Slaves of Maquinna.* Reprint of the 1815 text. Surrey, B.C.: Heritage House, 2000.

Jones, Charles. *Queesto-Pacheenaht Chief by Birthright.* Nanaimo: Theytus Books, 1981.

Kirk, Ruth. *Wisdom of the Elders.* Vancouver: Douglas & McIntyre, 1986.

Kozloff, Eugene N. *Seashore Life of the Northern Pacific Coast.* Seattle: University of Washington Press, 1983.

Leadem, Tim. *The West Coast Trail and Other Great Hikes.* Vancouver: Douglas & McIntyre, 1998.

Macfarlane, J.M., H.J. Quan, K.K. Uyeda and K.D. Wong. *The Official Guide to Pacific Rim National Park Reserve.* Calgary: Blackbird Naturgraphics, 1996.

McMillan, Alan D., and Eldon Yellowhorn. *First Peoples in Canada.* Vancouver: Douglas & McIntyre, 2004.

Mills, Donald C. *Giant Cedars, White Sands: The Juan de Fuca Marine Trail Guidebook.* Sooke, B.C.: Pallas Trine Services, 1999.

Nicholson, George. *Vancouver Island's West Coast 1762–1962.* Victoria: Morriss Printing Company, 1962.

Obee, Bruce. *The Pacific Rim Explorer.* North Vancouver: Whitecap Books, 1986.

Ormsby, Margaret A. *British Columbia: A History.* Toronto: The MacMillans in Canada, 1958.

Peterson, Lester. *The Cape Scott Story.* Vancouver: Mitchell Press, 1974.

Pethick, Derek. *First Approaches to the Northwest Coast.* Vancouver: Douglas & McIntyre, 1976.

——*The Nootka Connection.* Vancouver: Douglas & McIntyre, 1980.

Pojar, Jim, and Andy MacKinnon. *Plants of Coastal British Columbia.* Vancouver: Lone Pine Publishing, 1994.

Scott, R. Bruce. *Barkley Sound a History of the Pacific Rim National Park Area.* Victoria: Sono Nis Press, 1972.

——*Breakers Ahead!* Victoria: Sono Nis Press, 1970.

——*People of the Southwest Coast of Vancouver Island.* Victoria: Morriss Printing Company Ltd., 1974.

Sheldon, Ian. *Seashore of British Columbia.* Vancouver: Lone Pine Publishing, 1998.

Snively, Gloria. *Exploring the Seashore in British Columbia, Washington and Oregon.* West Vancouver: Gordon Soules Book Publishers, 1995.

Sound Heritage. *Nutka-Captain Cook and the Spanish Explorers on the Coast.* Province of British Columbia, 1978.

Stoltmann, Randy. *Hiking the Ancient Forests of British Columbia and Washington.* Vancouver: Lone Pine Publishing, 1996.

Varner, Collin. *Plants of the West Coast Trail.* Vancouver: Raincoast Books, 2002.

Walbran, John T. *British Columbia Coast Names.* Vancouver: Douglas & McIntyre, 1971.

Wells, R.E. *A Guide to Shipwrecks along the West Coast Trail.* Victoria: Sono Nis Press, 1981.

Rain Coast Chronicles, a series of annual volumes published by Harbour Publishing, is an excellent source for materials on the history of the west coast of Vancouver Island.

> **WEB SITES WITH VALUABLE INFORMATION:**

srmwww.gov.bc.ca/bcnames/
> Information on place names in British Columbia.

wlapwww.gov.bc.ca/bcparks/
> Important up-to-date information on B.C. Provincial Parks.

waterlevels.gc.ca/
> Information on tide tables, from the Web site of Canadian Hydrographic Services.

www.pc.gc.ca/pn-np/bc/pacificrim/
> Information on the West Coast Trail and Pacific Rim National Park Reserve.

weatheroffice.ec.gc.ca/forecast/canada/
> Information on current and upcoming weather forecasts.

www.alberni.net/quuas
> Information on the West Coast Trail, from the Web site of Quu'as West Coast Trail Society.

INDEX

. . . . .

Page numbers in *italics* refer to maps and illustrations.

access and permits: Cape Scott area, 125, 127; Carmanah Walbran, 78–80; Juan de Fuca Trail, 29–31, 35; Long Beach, 90–92; Nootka Trail, 110–11; West Coast Trail, 47–52
Adrenaline Creek, 63–64, 65
Ahousaht Band, 92, 106–8, 155
Ahousat village, 91–92, 106–7
Ahous Bay, 106
Amphitrite Point, 90, 93, 94–96
Anderson Lake, 85, 87, 88
Arch Rock, 36
Auger Lake, 85, 87, 88

Baird, Tom, 43
Bajo Point, 116, 117
Bamfield, *xii*, 50–53, 73, 75–76
Banfield, William, 52–53
BC Parks, 31, 34, 167
Beano Creek, 116–19, 121, 122
Bear Beach, 33, 34, 35
bears, 12–13, 40, 148
Big Beach, 93, 95, 96
Billy Goat Creek, 69, 72
Bodega y Quadra, Juan Francisco de la, 123
Bonilla Creek, 64, 65, 66
Bonilla Point, *vi*, 64, 65, 66

Botanical Beach, 31, 34, *41*, 43–44, 57
Botley Creek, 85, 87
Botley Lake, 85, 87, 88
Box Island, *101*, 103–4
Brown, Robert, 70
Bruce, Randolph, 124

cable cars, 15, 61
Callicum, 119
Callicum Creek, 119, *121*
Calvin Falls, 115, *117*
Camper Bay, 57, 59–62, 155
camping: campfires, 16, 22, 35, 83, 138; ethics and etiquette, 17–19, 54–55, 83, 155. *See also* equipment; *specific trails*
camping fees. *See* access and permits
Camp Patience, 84
Camp Perfection, 88
Cape Beale, 73, 76
Cape Palmerston, 127, 141–44
Cape Scott Provincial Park: access and permits, 125, 127; campsites, 127, 134–35, 138–39, 142; Eric Lake to Fisherman River, 135, *136*; Fisherman River to Cape Scott, 135–40; history, 128–31, 135, 138, 141; lighthouse, 140; maps, *xii*, 125, 133, *136*, *137*; ratings, 125, 126, 141; San Josef River to Eric Lake, 131–35; tide problems, 132; tide tables, 125

Captain Cook, 128
Carmanah Beach, 67
Carmanah Creek, 65, 66–67, 79
Carmanah Forestry Society, 79, 82, 84, 87
Carmanah Point, 63, 65, 66–67, 148
Carmanah Valley, 81, 82–84, 151
Carmanah Walbran Provincial Park:
    access and permits, 78–80; campsites,
    82–84, 87, 88; Carmanah Valley, 81,
    82–84, 151; history, 82, 159–60; maps,
    xii, 77, 79, 81, 85; ratings, 77, 78; safety
    concerns, 83–84; Walbran Valley, 79,
    84–88
Central Walbran Creek, 85, 87
Central Walbran Trail, 80, 85, 88
Cheewat River, 53, 65, 67–68, 69, 151
China Beach, 30, 33, 34, 35
Chin Beach, 36–38
Christensen family, 134–35
Cleland Island, 106
Clinch Creek, 33, 35–36
Clo-oose, 68, 70, 159
clothing, 24–26
Combers Beach, *101*, 103
conservation: ecosystem management,
    164–65; logging and coastal forests,
    157–59, 162–64; Nootka Trail protec-
    tion, 165, 167; public awareness,
    167–68; and recreation, 160, 162;
    species at risk, 152. *See also* forests;
    wildlife
Cook, James, 123
cougars, 13, 148
Cow Bay, 108, 149
Cowichan Lake, 78–79
Crawfish Lake, 115
Cribs, Bay of the, 67
Cullite Creek, 57, 159–60

Dare Point, 65, 67
Darling River, 73, 74–75
DesJarlais, Doug, 127

Ditidaht First Nation, 61, 68, 70, 153, 155
Doobah River, 151

ecosystems, 145–51, 160, 164–65
ecotourism. *See* recreation industry
equipment, 16–17, 19–26, 28
Eric Lake (Erie Lake), *133*, 134–35, *136*
Experiment, 128
Experiment Bight, 138

Ferrer Point, *113*, 114
ferries. *See* access and permits
Fetus Lake, 85, 87
First Nations, 139–40, 147, 153–56. *See
    also specific people and groups*
Fisherman Bay, 129, 137
Fisherman River, 135, 136, 137
Florencia Bay, 93, 97–99, 101
Florencia Beach, 97–99
Flores Island, 91–92, 104, 106–8, 149, 158
food, 19, 22, 27–28
forest industry. *See* logging
forests, 86, 130; blowdown, 164–65; con-
    servation of, 162–64; as ecosystems,
    145–51, 160, 164–65; multiple uses of,
    157–60; old growth, 80, 100, 162–64;
    wind pruning, 59, 61, 102. *See also*
    logging; trees
Forward, HM Gunboat, 98
Friendly Cove. *See* Yuquot
Fuca, Juan de, 32

Giggling Spruce grove, 87
Gold River, *xii*, 110
Gordon River, 56, 57, 58
"Graveyard of the Pacific", 31–32, 53. *See
    also* shipwrecks
Green Point, *101*, 103
Grove, William, 68
Grunt's Grove, 81, 83
Guise, John, 128
Guise Bay, *134*, 137, 138–39

174 | INDEX

Halfmoon Bay, 93, 97
Hanna, James, 132
Hansen, Rasmus, 128–29, 131
Hansen Lagoon, 128–29, 131, 137, 138
Haskell, Syd, 87
hazards: boardwalks, ladders and stairs,
    10, 14–15; drinking water, 27, 115; fixed
    ropes, 15; hypothermia, 11–12; logging
    trucks, 51, 78, 127; red tide, 151–52; sea
    hazards, 13–14, 63–64; stream cross-
    ings, 12, 14, 15–16, 18, 23–24, 83; surge
    channels, 63–64; terrain, 14–17, 35, 39;
    theft and vandalism, 31, 52; unmain-
    tained trails, 82–84; wildlife, 12–13. See
    also specific trails; tide problems
Hecht, Willie, 142
Hesquiaht Band, 105, 155
He-Tin-Kas Park, 93, 96
Hoard Creek, 33, 36, 37
Holberg, 127
Hole-in-the-Wall, 50, 71
Hot Springs Cove, 91–92, 104–6
Hummingbird Camp, 84
Huu-ay-aht First Nation, 61, 75, 153, 155
hypothermia, 11–12

Ivanhoe Creek, 33, 35

Jensen, N.P., 139
Jewitt, John, 123
Jewitt Lake (Aa-aak-quaksius Lake), 121, 123
Juan de Fuca Marine Trail, 146; access
    and permits, 29–31; campsites, 35–36,
    38–40, 43; China Bay to Magdalena
    Point, 33, 35–36; history, 31–32; Mag-
    dalena Point to Sombrio Bluffs,
    36–40; maps, 29, 33, 37, 41, 57; ratings,
    29, 30; Sombrio Bluffs to Botanical
    Beach, 40–44; tide problems, 34, 36,
    39; tide tables, 29

Keeha Bay, 73, 76
Kichha Lake, 73, 76

Kiutshe Cove, 40, 41
Kiutshe Creek, 40, 41
Krajina, Vladimir, 145
Kulaht Creek, 64, 65
Kwakwaka'wakw people, 153, 155–56

Ledingham Creek, 33, 36
Life Saving Trail, 31, 53
lighthouses, 63, 67, 90, 94–95, 124, 140
Lismer, Arthur, 102
Lismer Beach, 161
Lismer Cove, 102
Little Kiutshe Creek, 40, 41
Logan, David, 63, 68
Logan Creek, 10, 23, 57, 62–63, 65,
    159–60
logging: in coastal forests, 162–64; land
    use conflict, 32, 54, 157–59, 160; trucks
    on roads, 51, 78, 127
Log Jam Creek, 57, 58
Long Beach, 98; access and permits,
    89–92; campsites, 103, 105; Long
    Beach trails, 101, 102–4; maps, 89, 93,
    101; Quisitis Point trails, 99–102; rat-
    ings, 89, 94, 97, 99–100, 102, 104; tide
    tables, 89; Tofino area trails, 104–8;
    Wild Pacific Trail, 93, 94–97; Willow-
    brae Trail and Florencia Bay, 97–99.
    See also Pacific Rim National Park
Loss Creek, 37, 38–39
Lost Shoe Creek, 99
Louie Lagoon (Starfish Lagoon), 112, 113
Lowrie, Henry, 128
Lowrie Bay, 132–34

Maaktusiis, 91–92, 106–7
Macjack River, 129, 142
Magdalena Point, 33, 36
maps (figures). See specific trails and
    places
maps (topographic), 1–2; Cape Scott, 125;
    Carmanah Walbran, 77; Juan de Fuca

Trail, 29; Long Beach, 89; Nootka
    Trail, 109; West Coast Trail, 45–46
Maquinna, 100, 123
Maquinna, 124
Maquinna, Napoleon, 124
Maquinna Marine Park, 105–6
Maquinna Point, 120, *121*
marbled murrelets, 84, 151, 159
Martin, "Oyster Jim", 94
Merriman, Alec, 32
Michigan Creek, 72, 73, 75
Minute Creek, 39, 40, *41*
Mowachaht-Muchalaht First Nation, 111,
    112, 116, 155
Mowinis, 122
Mystic Beach, 33, 34, 35
Mystic's Hollow Camp, 84

Nahwitti-Shushartie corridor, 131, 141
Nels Bight, 135, *137*, 138
Nissen Bight, 135, *137*, 138
Nitinat Lake, 54, 69, 71, 78, 158–59
Nitinat Narrows, 14, 69, 70–71
Nitinat Triangle, 158–59
Nootka Convention, 123
Nootka Island, *xii*, 111–12, *118*, 123–24, 149
Nootka Trail, *18*, 25, *150*; access and per-
    mits, 109–11; Beano Creek to Friendly
    Cove, 119–24, *121*; campsites, 120, 122;
    history, 112, 116; Louie Lagoon to
    Skuna Bay, 112–15; maps, 109, *113*, *117*,
    121; protection of, 165, 167; ratings,
    109, 110; Skuna Bay to Beano Creek,
    115–16, *117*, 119; tide problems, 114–15,
    119, 120, 122; tide tables, 109
Nuu-chah-nulth First Nation: Flores
    Island, 106–8; history and culture, 100,
    147, 153, 155; Nootka Island, 111–12
Nuu-chah-nulth Trail, 99, 100, *101*, *166*

Ohlsen, Henry, 131, 132
150 Yard Creek, 57, 59

Openit Peninsula, 105
Orange Juice Creek, 73, 75
Owen Point, 57, 59

Pacheedaht First Nation: history, 153, 155;
    Quu'as, 61; trail building by, 44; West
    Coast Trail access, 52, 56, 58
Pachena Bay, 75, *162*
Pachena Point, 73, 75, 148
Pacific Rim National Park, *161*, 165, *166*;
    access and permits, 91; Long Beach
    Unit, 103–4; omissions from, 158–59;
    West Coast Trail Unit, 54; Willowbrae
    Trail, 97–99. *See also* Long Beach;
    West Coast Trail
Palmerston, Henry, 144
Paradise Pool, 81, 83
parking. *See* access and permits; *specific
    trails*
Parkinson Creek, 30–31, 40, 43
Payzant, Frederick, 43
Payzant Creek, *41*, 43
permits. *See* access and permits
plants, 146–48. *See also* trees
Port Alberni, *xii*, 50–51, 90–92
Port Renfrew, *xii*, 52, 57
potlatch, 156
Princess Royal, 39
Providence Cove, *41*, 43

Quatsino First Nation, 128, 156
Quimper, Manuel, 39
Quisitis Point, 99–102
Quu'as, 61, 68, 71, 155, 156

Radar Beach, 104
Raft Cove Provincial Park, 127, 141–42
Randy Stoltmann Commemorative
    Grove, 81, 83
recreation industry, 105, 157–62, 167. *See
    also* access and permits
Ronning, Bernt, 144

Ronning Gardens, *143*, 144
Ronning Mainline, 141, 144
Rosander Mainline, 81, 82
Rosemond Creek, 33, 35–36

St. Patrick, Mount, 132, *133*
Sandstone Creek, 57, 62
San Josef Bay, 131, 132, *133*
San Josef River, *136*, 137
San Simon Point, 33, 35
Schooner Cove Trail, *101*, 102–4, 165
Scott, David, 128
sea caves, 59, 120, *121*, 132
Sea Otter Cove, 132–34
Shelter Bight, 69, 72
shipwrecks, 31–32; *Cape Scott*, 134–35;
    at Clo-oose, 68; *D.L. Clinch*, 35–36;
    Florencia, 97–98; *Glafkos*, 96;
    Janet Cowan, 72; *Michigan*, 72;
    Nootka Trail, 114; *Pass of Melfort*, 96;
    Robert E. Lewers, 72; at Shelter B
    ight, 72; *Uzbekistan*, 74; *Valencia*,
    53, 63, 72
Sierra Club, 32, 54, 82
Sierra Legal Defence Fund, 32
Skuna Bay, *113*, 115
Sloan, Gordon, 157
Sombrio Beach, 30, 37, 38–39, 42
Sombrio Bluffs, 39–40
Sombrio Point, 37, 39
Sombrio River, 39–40
Soule, Annie, 43
Soule Creek, *41*, 43, 57
South Beach Trail, 99–102
Spencer, Alfred, 138
Stone, William, 68
Sutton, William, 99

Tapaltos Bay, 73, 76
Third Beach, *113*, 114–15
Thrasher Cove, 57, 58–59
tide problems: Cape Scott, 132; Juan de
Fuca Trail, 34, 36, 39; Long Beach,
103; Nootka Trail, 114, 119, 120, 122;
and stream crossings, 14; and time
estimates, 8; West Coast Trail, 55–56,
62–64, 71, 76
tide tables, 2–4, 12; Cape Scott, 125; Juan
de Fuca Trail, 29, 34; Long Beach, 89;
Nootka Trail, 109; West Coast Trail, 46
Tilden, Josephine, 44
Tla-o-qui-aht (Clayoquot) Band, 100, 155
Tlatlasikwala (Nahwitti) First Nation,
128, 156
Tofino area, *xii*, 90–92, 104–8.
    See also Long Beach; Pacific Rim
    National Park
Tom Baird Creek, *41*, 44, 57
Tongue Point, *113*, 114
trail etiquette, 17–19, 54–55, 155. *See also*
camping
trailheads. *See* access and permits
trail ratings, 4–8. *See also specific trails*
trees: Douglas-fir, 145, 163; Fallen Giant,
81, 83; Heaven Tree, 81, 83; Maxine's
Tree, 85, 87; red alder, 147; shore
pine, 147–48; Sitka spruce, 54, 82, 87,
103, 145, 147; Three Sisters, 81, 83; vine
maple, 147; western hemlock, 147;
western red cedar, 147; yellow-cedar,
148. *See also* forests
Trestle Creek, 69, 72
Trisle Creek, 57, 59
Tsa'tsil, 120, *121*, 122
Tsocowis Creek, 69, 72, 73, 75, 155
T'souke First Nation, 44
Tsuquadra Creek, 155
Tsuquadra First Nation, 71
Tsuquadra Point, 69
Tsusiat Falls, 70, 71–72
Tsusiat Point, 50, 69, 71

Ucluelet (Clayoquot) Band, 155
Ucluelet area, *xii*, 93, 94–99.

See also Long Beach; Pacific Rim National Park
Ucluth Peninsula, 93, 94–97

Vancouver, George, 123
Vancouver Point, 64, 65
Vargas Island, 91–92, 104, 106, 149

Walbran, John T., 64
Walbran Creek, 63–64, 65
Walbran Valley, 79, 84–88. *See also* Carmanah Walbran Provincial Park
weather, planning for, 16, 26
Web sites: Carmanah Forestry Society, 79; federal government, 152, 168; provincial government, 31, 34, 167, 168
West Coast Trail, *xii*, 74; access and permits, 45, 47–52, 55, 75, 83; campsites, 58–62, 64, 71–72, 74–75; Cheewat River to Tsocowis Creek, 68–71; conservation issues, 158–59; Gordon River to Logan Creek, 57, 58–63; history, 52–54, 70; Logan Creek to Cheewat River, 63–68; maps, 45–46, 57, 65, 69, 73; ratings, 45–47; tide problems, 55–56, 62, 63–64, 71, 76; tide tables, 46; Tsocowis Creek to Pachena Bay, 71–75; whale watching, 149
Western Canada Wilderness Committee, 82, 84, 108
West Walbran Trail, 80, 84, 85, 87–88
whales, 39, 106, 108, 148–49, 153
Whyac, 70
Wickaninnish Bay, *101*, 102
Wickaninnish Beach, *101*
Wickaninnish Trail, 99, 100, *101*, *166*
wilderness ethic, 17–19, 54–55, 83. *See also* conservation
wildlife: bears, 12–13, 40, 148; birds, 68, 84, 103–4, 138, 149, 151, 159; cougars, 13, 148; deer, *140*, 148;

marbled murrelets, 84, 151, 159; safety with, 12–13; salmon, 151, 160; sea lions, 39, 75, 99, *146*, 148; seals, 148; sea otters, 116, 123, 148; small mammals, 149; species at risk, 152; tide pools, 38, 44, 103; tours, 105; whales, 39, 106, 108, 148–49, 153; wolves, 13, 148
Wild Pacific Trail, 93, 94–97
Wild Side Trail, 92, 104, 106–8
Williams, Ray, 124
Williams, Sanford, 124
Willingdon, Lord, 124
Willowbrae Trail, 97–99
wolves, 13, 148
Wreck Bay. *See* Florencia Bay
Wya Point, 99

Yauh Creek, *41*, 43, 57
Yuquot, 110–11, 121, 123–24, 154
Yuquot Point, *121*
Yutlinuk First Nation, 128, 156

TIM LEADEM is a lawyer by profession and a member of the bar in British Columbia. An avid hiker and climber for more than 35 years, he has hiked in locations all over the globe, but especially in British Columbia and on Vancouver Island. The author of perennial best-seller *The West Coast Trail and Other Great Hikes,* he also holds a master's degree in zoology. He lives in North Saanich, British Columbia, Canada.